with best wishes

Maron & Igor WD.

Boxers

BOXERS
AN OWNER'S COMPANION

Ivor Ward-Davies

The Crowood Press

First published in 1991 by
The Crowood Press Ltd
Ramsbury, Marlborough
Wiltshire, SN8 2HR

This impression 1994

British Library Cataloguing-in-Publication Data

Ward-Davies, Ivor
  Boxers.
  1.Boxers (Dogs)
  I Title
  636.73

  ISBN   1 85223 263 3

Throughout this book, 'he', 'him' and 'his' have been used as
neutral pronouns, and refer to both males and females, be they
human or canine.

Printed and bound in Great Britain by
BPCC Hazell Books Ltd.
Member of BPCC Ltd.

Contents

	Preface	7
1	Why a Boxer?	9
2	History of the Boxer	13
3	The Modern Boxer	21
4	The Breed Standard	30
5	Getting Started	65
6	Breeding	72
7	Mating	82
8	Pregnancy and Whelping	87
9	Bringing up the Puppies	102
10	Choosing a Puppy	109
11	Training	123
12	Showing	136
13	Assessing the Boxer	142
14	Show Judging	147
15	Imports and Exports	156
16	Advertising	164
17	First Aid and Diseases	168
	Appendix 1	184
	Appendix 2	186
	Index	189

Preface

It is impossible to cover the entire spectrum of activities associated with dog breeding and showing within the limitations of a book of this nature. I have tried to include enough information to act as a useful introduction and to whet the appetite for more advanced reading. There has to be limitations in the contents and so, if I have missed any particular dogs of note, I apologize. Most of the photographs have been produced by me, some of the archival photos are not very good but are worthy of inclusion because of the subject's importance.

My special thanks go to the two people who made this book possible: my secretary, Mrs Rita Batstone, who typed the manuscript in her spare time and corrected my worst grammatical errors, and my life long gratitude to my wife, Marion, without whose hard work, enthusiasm, knowledge and love of all dogs, but especially of the Boxer, there would not have been a Winuwuk Kennel.

1

Why a Boxer?

There are well over a hundred breeds of dog. With so many choices, why should we decide that the Boxer is the dog we should most like to own? Many people ask themselves why they should buy a pedigree dog at all when cross-breeds are plentiful and cheap and when pure-breeds have suffered such bad television and press publicity in recent years. We have owned or bred many breeds from Boston Terriers to a Great Dane and, while running a boarding kennel for many years, we also became familiar with the characteristics of many other types of dog, including cross-breeds. Part of our boarding kennel was reserved as a rehabilitation centre for stray dogs brought in from the Animal Protection Society and the police dog-catchers. We did have a few pedigree dogs brought in but the wastage of cross-bred dogs was sheer heartbreak, many abandoned because they had grown too large, others through temperament problems.

Of course, we were at the sharp end and there are many thousands of perfectly stable, intelligent and delightful cross-breeds perfectly suited to their owners, but one of the main advantages of a pedigree dog is that you have a very good idea of what the grown dog will be like, both in looks and temperament. A very good friend of mine wanted to give a home to a small cross-bred puppy. At the time, we had a terrier-type bitch who had been found rearing a litter in an old discarded mattress in a field and so my friend happily took one of the tiny puppies. The dog grew and grew until it turned into a miniature grizzly bear with a disposition to match: it not only terrified the local dog population but also the local residents.

My main point is that if you intend to have a dog who will give you many years of enjoyment you can avoid some of the gamble and lessen the risks by choosing a specific breed, thus increasing the probability that the dog will suit you and your family.

Having made my case for pedigree dogs, I shall tell you why Boxers in particular are the ideal dogs for me, and you may decide

*Ch. Seefeld Holbien CD (ex)
demonstrating that a top
show dog can still possess
terrific power and vigour.*

they are the perfect breed for you. The most obvious attraction is the sheer good looks of the Boxer breed: a most distinctive head with an expression that mirrors the mood of the dog – full of mischief with his friends and yet most formidable when faced with a potential threat; the medium-size body is well balanced, full of strength and a degree of elegance stops any impression of coarseness; an arched neck gives nobility; the short, tight coat, richly coloured and set off by white markings, puts a quality finish to the whole. This is a dog who can hold his own in any show-ring competition.

Despite being a strong active dog with a past reputation as a gladiator, the Boxer's temperament is one key to the popularity of the breed. All our Boxers have been so good-natured: not one has ever shown any signs of aggression towards the family: our children have virtually learned to walk hanging onto a Boxer's stumpy tail and the dogs have treated them as if they were made of glass. Natural clowns, they are always ready for a rough and tumble and yet are sensitive enough to be aware of your moods.

However, this gentle, trustworthy dog has another side – he is one of the old Bull breeds and the courage and tenacity of his ancestors are still there. Most of us never see the other side of our much-loved

Boxers make natural guards. This one is suspicious of the photographer.

pets but those of us who have are usually thankful, for though the Boxer is not easily aroused, he is terrible in his anger when protecting his people or house and home from any threat. Actually, even when guarding, the Boxer's natural instinct is to intimidate rather than attack – we once returned to our home to find an intruder backed against a wall with our dog just daring him to move a muscle. We find that the dogs seem to be aware of their strength and power and do not abuse it.

2

History of the Boxer

There is a tendency to assume that the Boxer is a modern breed. In fact, dogs of the Boxer type have roots back to antiquity. The natural head of the dog tends towards the wolf or the jackal – a broad head and short strong muzzle is not typical of the original wild dogs. However, there is no doubt that even going back to times BC special breeds were developed as war dogs: these dogs had heavy heads, short powerful muzzles and great courage. They were so different to the fine-headed, lightly built hunting dogs that they must have been selectively bred.

The early war dog was called "Molossis" by the Assyrians and was also used as a fighting and companion dog. Many of the early tribes and nations, including Britain, bred this type of dog and these are the ancestors of the Bull breeds that include Mastiffs, English Bulldogs, Boxers and others.

This type of dog was greatly prized so we can imagine the proud owners mating their bitches to similar dogs in order to retain the type. There must have been selection because we know that cross breeding the Boxer instantly results in the loss of the distinctive head and muzzle.

As the years went by, these distinctive dogs were used for boar-hunting and for the barbarous sports of dog-fighting and bear-baiting. A very specific type of dog emerged: powerful, large headed with a strong muzzle and boundless courage. The generic name for these dogs became *Dogge* and these split into two types: the large, heavy *Bullenbeisser* which is the ancestor of the Mastiff breed and, when mated to the red large hound, the Great Dane; and the smaller Bullenbeisser, the ancestor of the Boxer and the English Bulldog plus most of the other Bull breeds.

The two *Bullenbeissers* were defined around 1630 as the *Danziger* or large type and the *Brabanter* or small type. A famous description of these dogs was written in 1720 and a condensed version states:

Alts Schecken, born 1889, registered as number 50 in the first stud book. Through his granddaughter, Meta v.d. Passage, his blood flows in all our Boxers' veins.

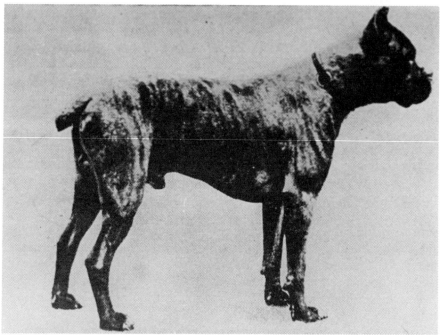

Ch. Gigerl, born 1901. An example of the early German foundation dogs. Gigerl was a prepotent brindle and helped to get rid of the whites and particolours.

The dogs have big heads and short, pushed-up noses; a broad head between their eyes; the ears and tails are clipped; most of them have short noses with a black muzzle and the lower jaw protrudes. They have black and yellow stripes and look vicious.

This old text certainly describes a dog of definite Boxer type. Many other early texts and drawings show the *Bullenbeisser* to be rich in Boxer characteristics. Many of these early descriptions asked for split muzzles or split upper lips – a problem we used to see in the Boxer but not so commonly nowadays.

The bull-baiting period did give the Boxer a dubious reputation but its use in the sport ensured that the breed was kept alive. While the German-type Bulldog kept its balance and reasonable length of leg, the British Bulldog (who was similar before selective breeding) developed into a very different type to the earlier Bulldog. The British Bulldog contributed to the development of the modern Boxer but this took place before the modern low-slung Bulldog evolved.

Bosko Immegrun, born 1898. Pictured here with his son Don Juan. In his time, he was rated very good and excellent in head. He is another ancestor of our modern Boxer.

The first Boxer Club was formed in Munich in 1896 and I suppose this marks the beginning of the Boxer breed as we know it. At this time, a standard was drawn up which has since been proved to have shown remarkable foresight and is the basis of our modern Standard. What really impresses me is that these old founders of the breed were describing a dog who did not yet exist in the flesh.

The Munich Boxer Club started a Stud Book; the breed was documented and, from them on, the history of the breed was available to the ardent pedigree student. It is noteworthy that, out of the breeding stock available in those early days, virtually every modern Boxer actually descends from relatively few dogs. The first great sire of the breed was a dog whelped in 1890, a golden brindle called Maier's

Ch. Rolf von Vogelsberg, born 1908. A great sire of his day, he inherited the Gigerl roach and tended to pass it on to his offspring. He was never beaten in the show ring and he served as a war dog during the 1914–18 War.

Lord – his blood runs in every Boxer's veins. The great dam of the breed was a rather ugly bitch called Meta v.d. Passage; another very important bitch was Mirzl. It was these bitches mated to three stud dogs, Flock St Salvator, Wotan and Bosco Immergrun whose descendants so dominated the breed that all other blood-lines virtually disappeared.

We must always remember that many of the breed's ancestors were white or particolour, and so should not be greatly surprised if we see an occasional white puppy appear in a litter. Another important dog was Ch. Gigerl, a solid brindle whelped in 1901. Gigerl was a dominant brindle and, through his descendants, played a large part in reducing the numbers of whites and particolours. Ch. Rigo v Angetor was a dark reddish fawn and showed a step forward in quality at that time: he was whelped in 1904 and was not only a great show dog, but sired thirteen Champions, which was a remarkable feat for Germany at that time. His sons did not make much impact at

Head study of Int. Ch. Dorian von Marienhoff, photographed in 1936.

17

Int. Ch. Sigurd von Dom of Barmere, born 1929, sire of twenty-six Champions. One of the four great imports that gave American Boxers such a good start.

stud; his influence on the breed was through his producing daughters. He also made the fawns so popular that they soon outnumbered the brindles. The balance was redressed when a great brindle Champion was born in 1908 – Rolf von Vogelsberg; he is described as tall for that time (nearly twenty-four inches at the withers), good head and neck, excellent shoulders and rear angulation, and he also had the roach back that was handed on from his great-grandfather, Ch. Gigerl. Rolf was a top working dog as well as a great show dog: he served through the First World War and returned to the ring at eleven years old to win his fifth Sieger title. Rolf was bought by Frau Stockmann and was a potent force in the establishment of the legendary Von Dom Kennel. Very few, if any, modern Boxers do not have Von Dom breeding in the pedigree. All real Boxer enthusiasts should beg, steal or borrow a copy of Frau Stockmann's book, *My Life with*

Int. Ch. Dorian von Marienhoff, sire of forty Champions.

Ch. Utz von Dom of Mazelaine, born 1933. The great German dogs of this time showed a great degree of elegance.

Int. Ch. Lustig von Dom of Tulgey Wood, born 1933. One of the key dogs in the breed, he had elegance and style and sired forty-one Champions.

Boxers; the line-drawings especially show the essence of the Boxer. One of Rolf's Sieger sons, Dampf v Dom went to the USA to become the first American Boxer Champion in 1915.

The first interest in the Boxer was aroused in the USA with the arrival of Ch. Check v Hunnenstein. This lovely dog was the first Boxer to win a Best in Show in America (this was in 1932 under the much respected Alva Rosenberg). This win really aroused interest and the Boxer started to become popular and was on its way to establishing itself as one of the USA's top dogs. The American Boxer also benefited from the importation of some of the greatest German dogs ever produced, notably: Int. Ch. Sigurd v Dom of Barmere, sire of twenty-six Champions; Int. Ch. Utz v Dom, sire of thirty-seven Champions; and Int. Ch. Dorian v Marienhof of Mazelaine, sire of forty Champions; and Int. Ch. Lustig v Dom of Tulgey Wood who sired forty-one Champions in the USA and had great impact on the British Boxer through his influential daughter, Alma v. d. Frankenwarte. These Boxers also made their mark at stud and show before they went to the USA.

There are often debates over German, British or American type but it should be remembered that all Boxers spring from the same source.

3

The Modern Boxer

Boxer history in the UK covers a comparatively short span when compared to our native breeds. The first British Champion, a dog called Horsa of Leith Hill, was made up in 1939. Horsa made no impact on the breed despite his good German breeding, possibly because of the lack of bitches to breed to him and the impact of the Second World War.

Following the war, British Boxers benefited from the arrival of Alma von der Frankenwarte, owned in partnership by Mrs E. Somerfield, Miss Mary Davis and Mrs Marion Fairbrother. Alma was a daughter of Lustig Von Dom, so the blood of this great dog came to Britain. Alma produced the bitch Ch. Panfield Serenade, sired by Juniper of Bramblings; and Ch. Panfield Tango, sired by Panfield Flak. Flak was Alma's grandson so we had line-breeding at the very start of the breed in the UK. The Panfield Kennel became one of the most influential in the early days and Mrs Somerfield was accepted as one of the breed's pioneers and a true Boxer expert. Other founders of the breed at this time were Mrs Marion Fairbrother (Gremlin), Mr Dawson (Stainburndorf), Mesdames Dunkels and Gamble (Breakstones), Mr and Mrs Dyson (Knowle Crest), Mr G. Jakeman (Immertreu), Mrs N. Hullock (Winkinglight).

The period from 1939 to 1960 was a really exciting time for Boxers. Many imports from Holland, Germany and the USA came to Britain and each played a significant role in the development of the British Boxer, which in turn was exported to various countries around the world. It is interesting to look back in history and see that relatively few dogs in Germany were the ancestors of our breed, how dominant the Von Dom breeding was, and how the blood-lines of a few dominant Boxers spread throughout the world and resulted in one of the most popular breeds. The early Boxers must have been very special dogs for their descendants to catch the attention of dog lovers in the way that they did.

Some of the great sires during this time were Dutch dogs: Ch.

Mazelaine's Texas Ranger, imported by the famous Panfield Kennels, and a brother to the great sire and show dog, Bangaway of Sirrah Crest. Texas Ranger sired five UK Champions.

Holger von Germania, who sired four Champions; Dutch Ch. Favourite Vom Haus Germania; Helios Vom Haus Germania (two Champions), Faust Vom Haus Germania (five Champions). These dogs came from the famous kennel of Mr Peter Zimmerman and had great influence on the breed. Mrs Hullock's important sires, Champion Winkinglight Justice and Viking had a predominantly Dutch background and were heavily involved in the background of the very successful Wardrobes' Kennels. We must not ignore the American influence: USA inputs such as Finemere's Flip of Berolina (two Champions), Am. Ch. Awldogg Southdown's Rector (two Champions), and the very important sire, the Panfield Kennel's Mazelaines Texas Ranger (five Champions) were also doing their bit to improve the breed. It is interesting to note that Texas Ranger was a full brother to another great sire, the American dog Ch. Bang Away of Sirrah Crest, another indication that good breeding pays off. Winkinglight sires were producing well in the 1950s: Felcign Faro produced four Champions and helped put Mrs F. Price's Kennels on the map.

At the end of the 1950s, a most important dog arrived from the USA, Mrs Fairbrother's and Mr M. Summers' Rainey Lane Sirocco, sire of thirteen Champions. The Wardrobes' sires were also very successful during this time. Following Sirocco, a most remarkable sire appeared: this super dog belonged to Mrs Pat Heath, and was called

Ch. Seefeld Picasso. His breeding is interesting – a combination of top American producers and lines back through the Winkinglight dogs to the original Dutch imports. The great Picasso sired eighteen UK Champions and a grand total of fifty-eight Champions worldwide. Not only a great sire but also a top show dog, Picasso won twenty-four CCs, one Best in Show and two reserve Best in Shows, five times Working Group winner at Championship Shows. At the time of writing, he is top British sire, but is now being challenged for his position by Miss S. Cartwright's Ch. Tyegarth Famous Grouse who has been the dominant sire of the 1980s. Grouse progeny are still in the ring although he himself has gone. Though he was a top-winning dog, he did not have the show-ring record of Picasso. I think it will be a very long time before we see a dog beat the records set by Picasso in his dual career as great show dog and great sire.

Picasso and Grouse, the dominant sires of their era, really bring us up to date. There were other excellent studs operating at this time,

Ch. Gremlin Summer Storm, UK's top-winning Boxer and also a dominant sire.

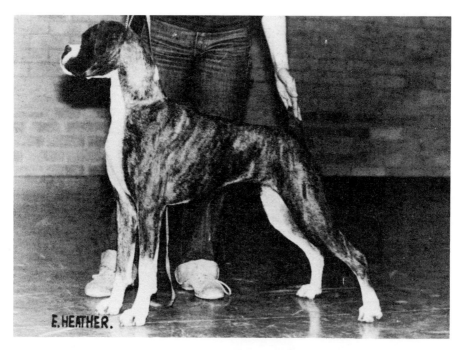

*Ch. Winuwuk Good Golly (twenty-five CCs). Twice British Boxer
Club Champion of Champions, and UK's top-winning brindle bitch.*

including Ch. Gremlin Summer Storm, the top-winning Boxer of all time in the UK. The super, red show and stud dog Ch. Starmark Sweet Talkin' Guy, our own American import Kreyons Back in Town of Winuwuk sired four UK Champions and Winuwuk Milray's Red Baron of Valvay has sired three. Back in Town sired Rainey Lane Grand Slam before leaving the USA and Slam went to Australia where he became a most successful sire himself. Red Baron had, during a relatively short period at stud, sired Ch. Winuwuk Good Golly who holds the UK record for top winning brindle bitch with twenty-five CCs. Both these dogs appear in many of the latest Champions' pedigrees, Golly took the record from another lovely brindle bitch, Mrs J. Malcolm's Ch. Skelder Burnt Almond.

I consider myself very fortunate to have known most of the early breeders, if only by showing dogs under them, and to have been educated in Boxers by some of these experts. Unfortunately, recent years have seen the demise of many of the breed's founders and the accumulated knowledge they possessed has gone for ever.

24

Ch. Steynmere Night Rider, sire of six UK Champions including three Championship Show Working Group winners.

Ch. Wardrobes Clair de Lune, the UK's top-winning bitch with thirty-one CCs.

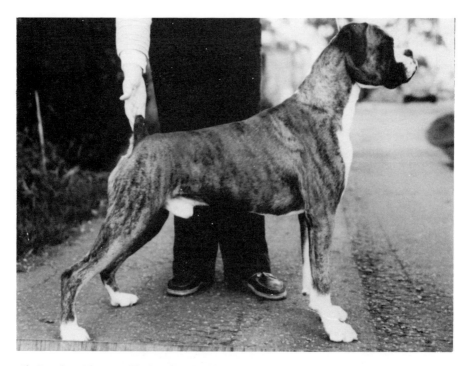

*Ch. Faerdorn Pheasant Plucker, Best in Show at All-Breed
Championship Show and also another influential sire.*

Many of the older established kennels continue up to the 1990s, including the Panfield's, which was one of the first Boxer kennels and is still going strong. Mrs P. Withers is still active with the Witherford Kennel. History was reversed when she sent her Ch. Witherford Hot Chestnut back to Germany where he proved a potent sire and set up a great record as a show dog. Another successful stud was Dr Cattanach's Ch. Steynmere Night Rider, one of the most successful products of this top kennel. Mr and Mrs J. Hambleton were producing top Boxers at this time, importing their lovely-headed dogs from the Continent and regularly producing top quality Champions. First of their most successful Boxers was the dark brindle Ch. Marbelton Desperate Dan who held the top-winning male Boxer record until overtaken by Ch. Gremlin Summer Storm. Then, amongst a steady stream of Champions came Ch. Marbelton Dressed to Kill who amassed twenty-six CCs, twice Best in Show, twice Reserve Best in Show and six times Working Group winner at All-Breed Championship Shows.

The present holder of the record for the greatest number of CCs for a bitch is the Wardrobes' bright red Ch. Wardrobes Clair de Lune with thirty-one CCs; Clair held the top Boxer title for some years. The Wardrobes' Kennel had also produced a great record-holding bitch and that was the legendary Miss Mink, a bitch who excelled in personality and ring presence. The Seefeld Kennel is still breeding and making up Champions. The long-established Braxburn Kennel of Mr and Mrs MacLaren is going strong in Scotland. The Faerdorns produced the super Ch. Faerdorn Pheasant Plucker, another top winner in breed and all-round competition. A close competitor who often fought it out with Pheasant Plucker was another superb dog, Mr and Mrs Banks' Ch. Norwatch Brock Buster: these dogs were hard to get past in the first half of the 1980s. Mr and Mrs Banks also owned the great producing bitch Norwatch Mustang Wine, whose UK record of five Champion progeny will be most difficult to beat. The Green-

Ch. Skelder Burnt Almond (twenty CCs). Championship Show Group winner.

ways' Rayfos Kennel had lots of success with many first-class Champions, Philip Greenway is certainly one of the top handlers in the UK. Daphne North's Carinya Kennel is still producing good ones. Peter Perret is still making up Champions with the Liedeberge prefix. Three other long-established kennels still breeding and showing good dogs are Miss J. Grover's Ackendenes, Mrs A. Kennett's Trywells and Mrs Foan's Ymars.

It is always good to see familiar faces and one of the areas where you can always see quality Boxers is the West Country where the Skelder, Kinbra, Tonantron, Klansted and Jimbren Kennels are situated. We have always seen good Boxers from the North: amongst the older, established kennels Mrs M. Best and her Wrencliffs have done some top winning. The Millers are having a lot of success with their winning dog, Ch. Jenroy Pop My Cork to Walkon. The Grouse brother, Ch. Tyegarth Glenmorangie of Jenroy is up amongst

Ch. Jenroy Pop My Cork to Walkon. A modern top winner in the UK with eighteen CCs who is also proving to be an outstanding sire.

Ch. Tyegarth Glenmorangie of Jenroy, sire of five Champions. Top Sire UK 1989.

the top sires for his owner Mrs J. Townshend. Mrs P. Broughton's Glenfalls and Mr and Mrs Zammit's Santonoaks have recently hit the high spots.

In Northern Ireland, Mrs and Miss Ingram's Tirkane Kennel is regularly making up Irish Champions; occasionally, they attend UK Championship Shows and pick up CCs.

There are many other breeders and dogs who have contributed significantly to the development of the Boxer. Unfortunately, space is limited, so I have not been able to mention them all.

4

The Breed Standard

The Breed Standard describes the characteristics of a breed. It is according to this Standard that a dog is judged or chosen for breeding; and it is towards producing this ideal that most breeders strive.

The first Boxer Standard was drawn up by the Boxer Club in Munich, known as the Deutscher Boxer Club, in January 1902 and was published in the first German Stud Book. Further revised in 1904, all subsequent Standards derive from this one, which is given below:

General Appearance

The general appearance of the Boxer is that of a short-haired, strong, compactly built, active, elegant dog, of medium height, standing on absolutely straight, sturdy legs and of perfectly square build.

The Head

The head should be dry throughout with as few wrinkles as possible. The cheeks should not be proportionately thicker than the upper part of the head, but instead should appear laterally compressed. The parallel lines of the muzzle should run directly forward, not tapering, so that the front of the muzzle forms a broad, square surface. The forehead is arched, the back of the head is high, the break of the forehead viewed from the side is definitely marked.

Upper and lower jaws are definitely parallel, the teeth at right angles to the jaws. The teeth of the lower jaw stand in front of the teeth of the upper jaw and fit so that the teeth touch each other when the mouth is closed, in the manner of scissors. The corner of the eye, which lies half-way between the nose and the occipital bone should not be pushed in under the forehead as it is in the Bulldog.

The nose is broad and black. The bridge of the nose is not broken but is straight. In front the lips are blunt; they should not hang over too much on the sides, just sufficiently covering the lower jaw. The teeth must be healthy and strong. The ears are set closely behind the cheekbone, trimmed to a point and carried erect. This as well as clipping of the tail is important because long ears give the dog a sleepy expression which is very objectionable. The eye is dark, of good size and full of life. A light eye is permissible in light-coloured animals.

Neck

The neck is strong, elegant, not too short, absolutely without dewlap, blending beautifully into the torso.

Body

The body is short, straight and rigid. The greatest emphasis should be placed upon these three qualities. The front is not broad but rather narrow. The chest deep but not wide, and absolutely must not hang between the elbows. The ribs should be well arched but not barrel-shaped, strong, with good tuck up. The hindquarters, legs and thighs are strong, muscular, powerful, not drooping. The kneecaps well rounded. Tail clipped, moderately high-set, gay, never carried above the back.

Legs and Paws

The legs are absolutely straight with strong bones. Paws small, round, closed. Soles strong, hard.

Coat and Colour

The hair is short and tight to the body. Basic colours of the Boxer are yellow and striped. These are the original colours. Yellow occurs in all different shades from wheaten to dark brown. White is not sought after as a basic colour but is permissible. It is not objectionable as a marking. A black mask improves the expression of yellow and striped Boxers.

Size

The height at the shoulders is between seventeen and twenty-two inches.

31

Defects

Coarse, Bulldog-like appearance. Loose shoulders. Off-standing elbows. Chest hanging between shoulders. Cow hocks. Weak or bad teeth. Double nose. Dewclaws. Long back. Too long or spread toes. Crossed teeth in the upper jaw or visible ones in the lower jaw. Flesh-coloured or brown nose. Flesh-coloured eyelids. Glass eye. Lack of temperament.

Qualities

The Boxer is alert, devoted, easily trained, with a very lively temperament. Never a bully, although his strength and agility enable him to compete successfully against any assailant. Famous as a defender of the person and property of his master. Boxers love water, are excellent retrievers and able ratters. A splendid companion and good room, house or estate dog.

To attain uniformity of judgement and guarantee the quickest arrival at correct Boxer type, the following outstanding breed characteristics are briefly specified in the order of their importance. General appearance. The three distinguishing marks of the back. Legs, paws and shoulders. Colour, the latter of the least importance, even if the basic colour is white, although in cases of otherwise equal qualification the Boxer with the least white would be preferable.

It is amazing how these early breeders drew up the Standard of a visionary animal, the challenge was to produce an active, elegant dog from the stock available at that time. These pioneers were very much aware of the Bulldog influence and tried to ensure that the Boxer did not carry forward the problem of the Bully type. We must always remember the efforts that were made to eliminate the ultra short foreface and exaggerated turn up of chin.

A number of Standards developed in different countries, the American version was drawn up by the American Boxer Club and approved by the American Kennel Club. I enjoy this version as it was obviously produced by Boxer lovers and goes a lot further than the usual basic requirements.

The American Breed Standard

(Reproduced by kind permission of
the American Kennel Club)

General Appearance

The Boxer is a medium-sized, sturdy dog, of square build, with short back, strong limbs, and short, tight-fitting coat. His musculation, well developed, should be clean, hard and appear smooth (not bulging) under taut skin. His movements should denote energy. The gait is firm yet elastic (springy), the stride free and ground-covering, the carriage proud and noble. Developed to serve the multiple purposes of guard, working and escort-dog, he must combine elegance with substance and ample power, not alone for beauty but to ensure the speed, dexterity and jumping ability essential to arduous hike, riding expedition, police or military duty. Only a body whose individual parts are built to withstand the most strenuous efforts, assembled as a complete harmonious whole, can respond to these combined demands. Therefore, to be at his highest efficiency he must never be plump or heavy, and, while equipped for great speed, he must never be racy.

The head imparts to the Boxer a unique individual stamp, peculiar to him alone. It must be in perfect proportion to the body, never small in comparison to the overall picture. The muzzle is his most distinctive feature, and great value is to be placed on its being of correct form and in absolute proper proportion to the skull.

In judging the Boxer, first consideration should be given to general appearance; next, overall balance, including the desired proportions of the individual parts of the body to each other, as well as the relation of substance to elegance – to which an attractive colour or arresting style may contribute. Special attention is to be devoted to the head, after which the dog's individual components are to be examined for their correct construction and function, and efficiency of gait evaluated.

General Faults Head not typical, plump, bulldoggy appearance, light bone, lack of balance, bad condition, lack of noble bearing.

Head

The beauty of the head depends upon the harmonious proportion of the muzzle to the skull. The muzzle should always appear powerful, never small in its relationship to the skull. The head should be clean, not showing deep wrinkles. Folds will normally appear upon the forehead when the ears are erect, and they are always indicated from the lower edge of the stop running downward on both sides of the muzzle. The dark mask is confined to the muzzle and is in distinct contrast to the colour of the head. Any extension of the mask to the skull, other than dark shading around the eyes, creates a sombre, undesirable appearance. When white replaces any of the black mask, the path of any upward extension should be between the eyes. The muzzle is powerfully developed in length, width and depth. It is not pointed, narrow, short or shallow. Its shape is influenced first through the formation of both jawbones, second through the placement of the teeth, and third through the texture of the lips.

The Boxer is normally undershot. Therefore, the lower jaw protrudes beyond the upper and curves slightly upward. The upper jaw is broad where attached to the skull and maintains this breadth except for a very slight tapering to the front. The incisor teeth of the lower jaw are in a straight line, the canines preferably up front in the same line to give the jaw the greatest possible width. The line of incisors in the upper jaw is slightly convex toward the front. The upper corner incisors should fit snugly back of the lower canine teeth on each side, reflecting the symmetry essential to the creation of a sound, non-slip bite.

The lips, which complete the formation of the muzzle, should meet evenly. The upper lip is thick and padded, filling out the frontal space created by the projection of the lower jaw. It rests on the edge of the lower lip and, laterally, is supported by the fangs (canines) of the lower jaw. Therefore, these fangs must stand far apart, and be of good length so that the front surface of the muzzle is broad and squarish and, when viewed from the side, forms an obtuse angle with the topline of the muzzle. Over-protrusion of the overlip or underlip is undesirable. The chin should be perceptible when viewed from the side as well as from the front without being over-repandous (rising above the bite line) as in the Bulldog. The Boxer must not show teeth or tongue when the mouth is closed. Excessive flews are not desirable.

The top of the skull is slightly arched, not rotund, flat, nor noticeably

34

broad, and the occiput not too pronounced. The forehead forms a distinct stop with the topline of the muzzle, which must not be forced back into the forehead like that of a Bulldog. It should not slant down (down-faced), nor should it be dished, although the tip of the nose should be somewhat higher than the root of the muzzle. The forehead shows just a slight furrow between the eyes. The cheeks, though covering powerful masseter muscles compatible with the strong set of teeth, should be relatively flat and not bulge, maintaining the clean lines of the skull. They taper into the muzzle in a slight, graceful curve. The ears are set at the highest points of the sides of the skull, cut rather long without too broad a shell, and are carried erect. The dark brown eyes, not too small, protruding or deep-set, are encircled by dark hair, and should impart an alert, intelligent expression. Their mood-mirroring quality combined with the mobile skin furrowing of the forehead gives the Boxer head its unique degree of expressiveness. The nose is broad and black, very slightly turned up; the nostrils broad, with the nasolabial line running between them down through the upper lip, which, however, must not be split.

Faults   Lack of nobility and expression, sombre face, unserviceable bite. Pinscher or Bulldog head, sloping topline of muzzle, muzzle too light for skull, too pointed a bite (snipy). Teeth or tongue showing with mouth closed, drivelling, split upper lip. Poor ear carriage, light ('Bird of Prey') eyes.

Neck

Round, of ample length, not too short; strong, muscular and clean throughout, without dewlap; distinctly marked nape with an elegant arch running down to the back.

Fault   Dewlap.

Body

In profile, the build is of square proportions in that a horizontal line from the front of the forechest to the rear projection of the upper thigh should equal a vertical line dropped from the top of the withers to the ground.

Chest and Forequarters

The brisket is deep, reaching down to the elbows; the depth of the body at the lowest point of the brisket equals half the height of the dog at the withers. The ribs, extending far to the rear, are well arched but not barrel-shaped. Chest of fair width and forechest well defined, being easily visible from the side. The loins are short and muscular; the lower stomach line, lightly tucked up, blends into a graceful curve to the rear. The shoulders are long and sloping, close-lying and not excessively covered with muscle. The upper arm is long, closely approaching a right angle to the shoulder blade. The forelegs, viewed from the front, are straight, stand parallel to each other, and have strong, firmly joined bones. The elbows should not press too closely to the chest wall or stand off visibly from it. The forearm is straight, long and firmly muscled. The pastern joint is clearly defined but not distended. The pastern is strong and distinct, slightly slanting, but standing almost perpendicular to the ground. The dewclaws may be removed as a safety precaution. Feet should be compact, turning neither in nor out, with tightly arched toes (cat feet) and tough pads.

Faults Chest too broad, too shallow or too deep in front; loose or overmuscled shoulders; chest hanging between shoulders; tied-in or bowed-out elbows; turned feet; hare feet; hollow flanks; hanging stomach.

Back

The withers should be clearly defined as the highest point of the back; the whole back short, straight and muscular with a firm topline.

Faults Roach back, sway back, thin lean back, long narrow loins, weak union with croup.

Hindquarters

Strongly muscled with angulation in balance with that of forequarters. The thighs broad and curved, the breech musculature hard and strongly developed. Croup slightly sloped, flat and broad. Tail attachment high rather than low. Tail clipped, carried upward. Pelvis long and, in females especially, broad. Upper and lower thigh long, leg well angulated with a clearly defined, well-let-down hock joint. In standing position, the leg below the hock joint (metatarsus) should be practically perpendicular to the ground, with a slight rearward slope permissible. Viewed from behind, the hind legs should be straight, with the hock joints leaning neither in nor out. The metatarsus should be short, clean and strong, supported by powerful rear pads. The rear toes just a little longer than the front toes, but similar in all other respects. Dewclaws, if any, may be removed.

Faults   Too rounded, too narrow, or falling off of croup; low-set tail; higher in back than in front; steep, stiff, or too slightly angulated hindquarters; light thighs; bowed or crooked legs; cowhocks; over-angulated hock joints (sickle hocks); long metatarsus (high hocks); hare feet; hindquarters too far under or too far behind.

Gait

Viewed from the side, proper front and rear angulation is manifested in a smoothly efficient, level-backed, ground-covering stride with powerful drive emanating from a freely operating rear. Although the front legs do not contribute impelling power, adequate "reach" should be evident to prevent interference, overlap or "side-winding" (crabbing). Viewed from the front, the shoulders should remain trim and the elbows not flare out. The legs are parallel until gaiting narrows the track in proportion to increasing speed, then the legs come in under the body but should never cross. The line from the shoulder down through the leg should remain straight, although not necessarily perpendicular to the ground. Viewed from the rear, a Boxer's breech should not roll. The hind feet should "dig in" and track relatively true with the front. Again, as speed increases, the normally broad rear track will become narrower.

Faults   Stilted or inefficient gait, pounding, paddling or flailing out of front legs, rolling or waddling gait, tottering hock joints, crossing over or interference – front or rear, lack of smoothness.

Height

Adult males – 22½ to 25 inches; females – 21 to 23½ inches at the withers. Males should not go under the minimum nor females over the maximum.

Coat

Short, shiny, lying smooth and tight to the body.

Colour

The colours are fawn and brindle. Fawn in various shades from light tan to dark deer red or mahogany, the deeper colours preferred. The brindle variety should have clearly defined black stripes on fawn background. White markings on fawn or brindle dogs are not to be rejected and are often very attractive, but must be limited to one third of the ground colour and are not desirable on the back of the torso proper. On the face, white may replace a part or all of the otherwise essential black mask. However, these white markings should be of such distribution as to enhance and not detract from the true Boxer expression.

Character and Temperament

These are of paramount importance in the Boxer. Instinctively a 'hearing' guard dog, his bearing is alert, dignified and self-assured, even at rest. In the show ring, his behaviour should exhibit constrained animation. With family and friends, his temperament is fundamentally playful, yet patient and stoical with children. Deliberate and wary with strangers, he will exhibit curiosity, but, most importantly, fearless courage and tenacity if threatened. However, he responds promptly to friendly overtures when honestly rendered. His intelligence, loyal affection and tractability to discipline makes him a highly desirable companion.

Faults Lack of dignity and alertness, shyness, cowardice, treachery and viciousness (belligerency toward other dogs should not be considered viciousness).

Disqualifications

Boxers with white or black ground colour, or entirely white or black, or any colour other than fawn or brindle. (White markings, when present, must not exceed one third of the ground colour.)

Approved December 12, 1967

38

For comparison the FCI Boxer Standard No. 144b is given below:
    Drawn up in 1905, this Standard was revised in 1920. In 1925 black
and white Boxers were excluded, in 1938 checks (parti-colours).

(Reproduced by kind permission of the
Federation Cynologique Internationale)

General Appearance

The Boxer is a medium-sized, smooth-haired, sturdy dog of short,
square build and strong bone. The musculation is clean (dry) and
powerfully developed and stands out plastically (pliantly) through
the skin. The movements are lively and full of strength and nobility.
The Boxer should not appear plump or heavy, lean or racy.

Head

The head imparts to the Boxer a unique, individual stamp. It must be
in good proportion to the body and should appear neither too light
nor too heavy. The skull should be as lean and angular as possible,
without salient cheeks, the muzzle as broad and massive as possible.
The beauty of the head depends on the harmonious proportion between the muzzle and the skull. From whatever direction the head is
viewed, whether from the front, from the top or from the side, the
muzzle must always appear in correct relationship to the skull, that
is, it must never seem too small. It should be clean (dry), showing
neither wrinkles nor dewlap. Folds normally appear on the forehead
when the ears are erect and they are always indicated from the root of
the nose running downward on both sides of the muzzle. The dark
mask is confined to the muzzle and must be in distinct contrast to the
colour of the head, so that the face will not have a sombre expression.
    The muzzle is powerfully developed in all three dimensions, thus it
must not be pointed or narrow, short or shallow. Its shape is influenced first through the formation of both jawbones, second through
the placement of the teeth in the jawbones and third through the
quality of the lips.
    The two jawbones do not end in a perpendicular plane in front, but
the lower jaw protrudes beyond the upper and curves slightly upward. The Boxer is normally undershot. The upper jaw is broad

39

where attached to the skull and maintains this breadth, except for a very slightly tapering to the front. Thus both jaws are very wide in front. The canine teeth should be as widely separated as possible, the incisors (6) should all be in one row, with no projection of the middle teeth. In the upper jaw they are set in a line curving slightly forward, in the lower jaw they should be in a straight line. The bite is powerful and sound, the teeth set in the most normal arrangement possible.

The shape of the muzzle is completed by the lips. The upper lip is thick and padded, filling out the frontal space created by the projection of the lower jaw and is supported by the fangs (canines) of the lower jaw. These fangs must therefore stand as far apart as possible and be of good length so that the front surface of the muzzle becomes almost square, forming an obtuse angle with the topline of the muzzle. The lower edge of the upper lip rests on the edge of the lower lip. The repandous part of the lower jaw, with the lower lip, called the chin, must not rise in front of the upper lip, but even less may it disappear under it. It must however be plainly perceptible when viewed from the front as well as from the side, without protruding and bending upward as in the Bulldog. The teeth of the lower jaw must not be visible when the mouth is closed, neither should the Boxer show its tongue when the mouth is closed.

The top of the skull is slightly arched, not so short as to be rotund, nor too flat, nor too broad and the occiput not too pronounced. The forehead forms a distinct stop with the topline of the muzzle. The bridge of the nose should not be forced back into the forehead like that of the Bulldog, nor should it slope down, however. The proportion between the length of the nose and that of the skull is as one (1) is to two (2). The tip of the nose lies somewhat higher than the root of the muzzle. The forehead shows a suggestion of furrow which however should not be too deep, especially between the eyes. The cheeks are powerfully developed to correspond with the strong bite, without protruding from the head with too bulgy an appearance. They should preferably taper into the muzzle in a slight curve. The ears are set on high, are cropped to a sharp point, fairly long, without too broad a shell and are carried perpendicular. The eyes are dark, not too small or protruding and not deep set. They disclose an expression of energy and intelligence but should not appear gloomy, threatening or piercing. The eyes must have a dark rim. The nose is broad and black, very slightly turned up, the nostrils wide, with the naso-labial line between them.

Faults Lack of nobility and expression, sombre face, unserviceable bite due to disease or faulty tooth placement, Pinscher or Bulldog head, drivelling, badly cropped ears, unpigmented third eyelid, showing teeth or tongue, light (bird of prey) eyes, sloping topline of the muzzle (downface), snipy bite or muzzle too light, brown, flesh-coloured or pink nose.

Neck

Round, not too short and thick but of ample length, yet strong, muscular and clean cut throughout, without dewlap. It runs down to the back in an elegant arch with distinctly marked nape.

Faults Dewlap.

Body

The build is square. The profile or outline, that is a horizontal line over the back and two vertical lines, the one touching the forechest in front, the other the ischiatic bones in the rear, form with the ground level a square. The torso rests on sturdy, straight legs with strong bones.

Chest and Forequarters

The chest is deep, reaching to the elbows. The depth of the chest amounts to half the height of the dog at the withers. The ribs are well arched but not barrel shaped, extending far to the rear. The loins are short, closed and taut and slightly tucked up. The lower stomach line blends into an elegant curve to the rear. The shoulders are long and sloping, close lying but not excessively covered with muscle. The upper arm is long, forming a right angle to the shoulder blade. The forelegs when seen from the front must be straight, stand parallel to each other and have strong, firmly articulated bones. The elbows must not press too closely to the chest wall nor stand off too far. The forearm is perpendicular, long and firmly muscled. The pastern joint of the foreleg is short, clearly defined but not distended. The pastern is short, slightly slanting but stands almost perpendicular to the ground. Feet are small with tightly arched toes (cat feet) and hard soles.

Faults Too broad and low in front, loose shoulders, chest hanging between the shoulders, hare feet, hollow flanks, hanging stomach, turned legs and toes.

Back

The withers should be clearly defined; the whole back short, straight, broad and strongly muscled.

Faults   Carp (roach) back, sway back, thin, lean back, long, narrow sharp sunken in loins, weak union with croup.

Hindquarters

Very strongly muscled, the musculation hard as a board and standing out very plastically (pliantly) through the skin. The thighs are not narrow and flat but are broad and curved. The breech musculation is as strongly developed. The croup slightly sloped, with a flat arch and broad. Tail set on high rather than too low, tail docked and carried upward. The pelvis should be long and, in bitches especially, broad. Upper and lower thigh long, hip and knee joint with as much angle as possible. In a standing position the knee should reach so far forward that it would meet a vertical line drawn from the hip protuberance to the floor. The hock angle about 140°, the lower part of the foot at a slight slope of 95–100° to the floor, thus not completely vertical. Seen from behind the hind legs should be straight. The hock joints clean, not distended, with powerful heels, the toes normally slightly longer than in front but similar in all other respects.

Faults   Falling off or too arched or narrow croup, low set tail, over-built (higher in back than in front), steep, stiff, insufficiently angulated hindquarters, light thighs, cow hocks, bow or sickle legs, narrow heels, hind dewclaws, soft hocks, tottering, waddling gait, hare feet, hindquarters too far under or too far behind.

Height

Males 56–63cm at the withers, females 53–59cm. The height is measured with the dog standing erect and the measurement is taken with a straightedge from the withers, down to the ground.

Mass

A male of about 60cm should be over 30kg, females of about 56cm should weigh about 25kg.

Coat

Short and glossy, lying smooth and tight to the body.

Colour

The colours are fawn and brindle. Fawn occurs in various shades, from dark deer red to light yellow, the shades in between (red fawn) are however the most beautiful. The mask is black, but must be confined to the muzzle so that the face does not appear sombre or unfriendly.

The brindle variety has dark or black stripes running parallel to the ribs, on a fawn ground colour in the above shades. The stripes should be in distinct contrast to the ground colour, neither too close together nor too thinly dispersed. The ground colour must not be dirty and the two colours should not be intermingled (grizzled) so that the brindle markings disappear.

White markings are not to be rejected; they are often very attractive in appearance. Unattractive white markings, such as a completely or laterally white head, etc., are faults.

All Boxers with any other colour, as well as those with the ground colour more than one third replaced by white, are not according to Standard.

Character

The character of the Boxer is of the greatest importance and demands the most solicitous attention. He is renowned from olden times for his great love and loyalty for his master and the whole household, his alertness and fearless courage as a defender and protector. He is harmless in the family but distrustful of strangers, bright and friendly of temperament at play, but fearsome when roused. He is easily trained due to his obedience, his self-assurance and courage, his natural sharpness and scenting ability. Because of his modesty and cleanliness he is equally desirable as a family dog and a guard, escort or service dog. He is honest and loyal, never false or treacherous even in his old age.

Faults Viciousness, treachery, unreliability, lack of temperament and cowardice.

The UK Breed Standard

(Reproduced by kind permission
of the Kennel Club of Great Britain)

General Appearance

Great nobility, smooth coated, medium sized, square build, strong bone and evident, well developed muscles.

Characteristics

Lively, strong, loyal to owner and family, but distrustful of strangers. Obedient, friendly at play, but with guarding instinct.

Temperament

Equable, biddable, fearless, self-assured.

Head and Skull

Head imparts its unique individual stamp and is in proportion to body, appearing neither light nor too heavy. Skull lean without exaggerated cheek muscles. Muzzle broad, deep and powerful, never narrow, pointed, short or shallow. Balance of skull and muzzle essential, with muzzle never appearing small, viewed from any angle. Skull cleanly covered, showing no wrinkle, except when alerted. Creases present from root of nose running down sides of muzzle. Dark mask confined to muzzle, distinctly contrasting with colour of head, even when white is present. Lower jaw undershot, curving slightly upward. Upper jaw broad where attached to skull, tapering very slightly to front. Muzzle shape completed by upper lips, thick and well padded, supported by well separated canine teeth of lower jaw. Lower edge of upper lip rests on edge of lower lip, so that chin is clearly perceptible when viewed from front or side. Lower jaw never to obscure front of upper lip, neither should teeth nor tongue be visible when mouth closed. Top of skull slightly arched, not rounded, nor too flat and broad. Occiput not too pronounced. Distinct stop, bridge of nose never forced back into forehead, nor should it be downfaced. Length of muzzle measured from tip of nose to inside corner of eye is one third length of head measured from tip of nose to occiput. Nose broad, black, slightly turned up, wide nostrils with well defined line between. Tip of nose set slightly higher than root of muzzle. Cheeks powerfully developed, never bulging.

Eyes

Dark brown, forward looking, not too small, protruding or deeply set. Showing lively intelligent expression. Dark rims with good pigmentation showing no haw.

Ears

Moderate size, thin, set wide apart on highest part of skull lying flat and close to cheek in repose, but falling forward with definite crease when alert.

Mouth

Undershot jaw, canines set wide apart with incisors (6) in straight line in lower jaw. In upper jaw set in line curving slightly forward. Bite powerful and sound, with teeth set in normal arrangement.

Neck

Round, of ample length, strong, muscular, clean cut, no dewlap. Distinctly marked nape and elegant arch down to withers.

Forequarters

Shoulders long and sloping, close lying, not excessively covered with muscle. Upper arm long, making right angle to shoulder blade. Forelegs seen from front, straight, parallel, with strong bone. Elbows not too close or standing too far from chest wall. Forearms perpendicular, long and firmly muscled. Pasterns short, clearly defined, but not distended, slightly slanted.

Body

In profile square, length from forechest to rear of upper thigh equal to height at withers. Chest deep, reaching to elbows. Depth of chest half height at withers. Ribs well arched, not barrel shaped, extending well to rear. Withers clearly defined. Back short, straight, slightly sloping, broad and strongly muscled. Loin short, well tucked up and taut. Lower abdominal line blends into curve to rear.

Hindquarters

Very strong with muscles hard and standing out noticeably under skin. Thighs broad and curved. Broad croup slightly sloped, with flat, broad arch. Pelvis long and broad. Upper and lower thigh long. Good hind angulation, when standing, the stifle is directly under the hip protuberance. Seen from side, leg from hock joint to foot not quite vertical. Seen from behind, legs straight, hock joints clean, with powerful rear pads.

Feet

Front feet small and catlike, with well arched toes, and hard pads; hind feet slightly longer.

Tail

Set on high, customarily docked and carried upward.

Gait/Movement

Strong, powerful with noble bearing, reaching well forward, and with driving action of hindquarters. In profile, stride free and ground covering.

Coat

Short, glossy, smooth and tight to body.

Colour

Fawn or brindle. White markings acceptable not exceeding one third of ground colour.

Fawn   Various shades from dark red to light fawn.

Brindle Black stripes on previously described fawn shades, running parallel to ribs all over body. Stripes contrast distinctly to ground colour, neither too close nor too thinly dispersed. Ground colour clear not intermingling with stripes.

Size

Height: Dogs 57–63cms (22½–25ins); Bitches: 53–59cms (21–23ins). Weight: Dogs approximately 30–32kg (66–70lbs); Bitches approximately 25–27kg (55–60lbs).

Faults

Any departure from the foregoing points should be considered a fault and the seriousness with which the fault should be regarded should be in exact proportion to its degree.

Note Male animals should have two apparently normal testicles fully descended into the scrotum.

The UK Standard is a condensed version of the FCI Standard. It will be noted that the requirement for elegance has gone. I hope that the mental image of the Boxer as defined by the originators of the breed will not be changed to suit some modern fancy; that would be a most retrogressive step.

Interpretation of the Standard

If we cross-breed the Boxer to other breeds or to non-pedigree dogs, the first thing we lose is the distinctive head: the blunt muzzle disappears and is replaced by the longer and more tapered muzzle. This rapid loss of breed type indicates that the Boxer is a variation to the normal canine type and we are setting ourselves quite a difficult task when we decide that we want to breed good Boxers.

The Standard tells us the characteristics we should be breeding for, but how was the Standard developed? The important point to remember is that one of the original uses of the breed was to bait bulls; and this barbaric sport required a dog of great courage and agility. The aim was for the dog to grip the bull by the nose and to hang on until the bull was subdued. Time showed that particular characteristics

Lovely head study of Ch. Tyegarth Blue Kiwi.

helped the dog to become more and more efficient at bull-baiting and owners breeding for these required characteristics gradually evolved a type of dog that showed itself to be superior to other dogs when taking part in this dubious sport. The early breeders came to an agreement on the required points, put these onto paper and prepared the first Breed Standard for the Boxer. When we judge the breed, and we are always judging the breed either in our own kennels or in the show ring, we should always remember the basic use of the Boxer and understand the importance of the points of the breed.

Head

Perhaps the most important and difficult breed characteristic is the head, so we will analyse the Boxer head and see how its original use has developed the unique head of the breed. The Boxer required great gripping power and so the undershot mouth was evolved. Most other breeds ask for a scissor bite with the lower incisors fitting neatly behind the upper incisors; we reverse this requirement for the Boxer.

Many of the other breeds rip and slash when fighting but the Boxer grips and holds on until its opponent is subdued. The mechanics of the undershot lower jaw give efficient gripping when the weight of the dog is suspended by the jaws, the upper teeth act as a fulcrum driving the lower teeth in. However, the grip is not so efficient when the dog's weight is thrown upwards and this can explain why the early prints of bull-baiting show the handlers busily catching the dogs as they were thrown upwards when the bull tosses its head. The dogs were used in relays until the bull tired out and a dog successfully

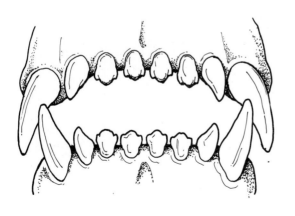

Correct mouth: the line of the lower teeth is straight while the line of the upper teeth is slightly curved. Incisors of good size and separated.

pinned it. As the dog most likely to be successful in the final pin was the one with an undershot jaw, such a jaw became a very important feature of the Boxer. The lower jaw must be slightly turned up to get the correct fit between the upper and lower incisors, which, again, means that the Boxer has a definite chin. The jaws should be as wide as possible and maximum width is achieved when the lower incisors and canine teeth are set in a straight line. We must always keep in mind that the jaw is designed to grip rather than to bite out a chunk and so width is necessary. A similar comparison can be made between a pair of pliers and a pair of scissors: pliers have a broad jaw for gripping; scissors are narrow for cutting.

The correct mouth and bite need to be understood because this has a crucial effect on the whole head. If the dog has width without the required turn up, the muzzle never looks correct; it tends to look long and often the whole head looks too fine and out of proportion. If the jaw is too undershot, we often get too much turn up; the muzzle tends to shortness and the whole head looks too wide. There are definite indicators that muzzles that are too short and wide lead to

American Ch. Notelracs Major Beau. A beautiful American head.

Xeno von der Glockenbergen, at eight years old. Outstanding sire in Germany, especially in producing head type.

51

Ch. Grysett von der Goldquelle, top-winning brindle bitch (Germany 1986–1988).

degeneration and a reduction in the number of lower incisors. This is shown in the extreme by some toy breeds that ask for a very wide muzzle. There is a general lack of understanding that the Boxer's jaw is normally undershot. Most breeders have at some time been contacted by a furious veterinarian complaining that a customer has been sold a puppy with a congenital defect, that is, an undershot jaw.

The requirement for a powerful grip sets up the rest of the head. The correct mouth defines the shape of the muzzle, which should be wide, deep and powerful. The width must be given by bone structure; some muzzles look good until you physically feel for width and you find that the muzzle is mostly made up of skin and padding. Some padding is required because the undershot jaw needs a padded upper lip to give the blunt finish to the muzzle that the Standard calls for.

The strong muzzle needs a powerful skull to operate it, we do not

Ch. Coebes von Westfalenwappen who possesses a lovely German head and is very successful in Working Trials.

want a coarse head so the skull and muzzle should be roughly balanced and the side skull should be smoothly curved into the muzzle.

The Boxer is a direct dog, direct in character and direct in his attack; he does not need the peripheral vision of a sight hound so the eyes are set into the skull so that he looks straight ahead. This type of eye setting requires room and this is provided by the distinct stop or break between the muzzle and top skull. This distinct stop must always be apparent when examining the head from the side. Rise of skull is also a requirement and any lack of stop and rise of skull will make the head tend towards the Great Dane type; and excess in both points will lead to the Boston Terrier type head. The Dane type head is not so common in modern dogs. We also breed Boston Terriers and see a Boxer's tendency towards the Boston head that is more obvious to Boston breeders.

One measurement in the Boxer head is quite specific: the muzzle makes up one third of the total length of the head including the

Ch. Lacoste von Ellinghaus,
top-winning fawn bitch
(Germany 1986–1988).

Gayus Von Schatzkastlein. German dog who was the European top
winner during the mid-seventies.

Quinto Manalito Von der Klappeheide of Marbelton (Dutch import).

Dolf the Buhe Farm of
Marbelton (Dutch import).

muzzle. Unfortunately, this measurement can be retained even if the whole head is too long or too short and this is the root cause of a whole series of problems and national variations in type. We do not want a lean skull; we want a clean skull. The Boxer needs an ample brain pan to retain his intelligence and reasoning power, the olden day bull-baiter went through a rigorous selection procedure: if they were not clever enough, the bull declared them permanently redundant; the ones who survived were intelligent and we want to retain that intelligence. There is no real problem with this. If we breed the required strong muzzle we must have an acceptable width of skull. What we want is a clean skull, no lumpy cheek muscles, no excessive wrinkles; and apple heads with narrow, weak muzzles are definitely out.

The whole attraction of the Boxer head is its unique expression and there are other points that are essential to give that special appeal. If the eyes are the mirror of the soul, this is especially true with the Boxer. We need an eye that shows the essential character of the breed.

Ch. Kinbra Uncle Sam of Winuwuk (thirteen CCs). Top male Boxer (UK 1977).

A small or oblique eye gives an impression of meanness; a light eye gives a hard expression; a round, bold eye totally ruins expression. The Boxer eye should be generous, dark and lozenge shaped. We like a big black nose with open nostrils. This, with a slight layback, allowed the dog to breathe freely when gripping. A slightly tilted nose tip ensures that the nose is higher than the root of the muzzle, a point sometimes lacking with modern dogs. The folds at the root of the muzzle coupled with the deep stop also ensured that the blood from the bull's nose was kept out of the dog's eyes, not a pleasant subject but we are looking at the distant history of the breed and trying to understand why specific details in the Standard are there. Heads are difficult but they are the hallmark of the breed, the best way to learn the correct head type is to look at the top-winning dogs and study head photographs. Once you learn the correct expression it is unmistakable. A truly lovely head is an indication that the proportions are correct on the outside and inside of the head; you will easily recognize the untypical head and your only problem is to decide exactly what is wrong with it!

Neck

A Boxer's neck needs reach and flexibility so ample length is required. But we also need it to show strength and to be round with no loose skin (dewlaps). It should show a distinct crest and fit smoothly into the body. The correct neck makes a great contribution to the nobility that the breed must possess.

At this point, we should consider a change of purpose for the Boxer. The horrific sport of bull-baiting was banned and, to some extent, the rough and tough dogs bred for the sport were made redundant. However, the old fanciers were reluctant to see these distinctive dogs of great courage die out so their use was modified to general purpose, suitable as a guard and companion dog. The fearsome gladiator now needed smartening up. The distinctive head

Int. Nord. Uch Slch LP Korad Count on Barro. Swedish Show and Obedience Champion.

qualities and character were to be retained but more emphasis was placed on construction and mobility to enable the dog to accompany his owner during activities such as hiking, cycling and horse riding. The Boxer also found a new role as police and war dogs. In those early days, the old German fanciers produced a Standard that showed great foresight in laying down a specification that resulted in the handsome dogs we have today.

Forequarters

The neck must smoothly fit into the shoulders, which in itself asks for perfect shoulder placement. The shoulder-blades must be well laid back to give them the correct length. The forelegs should be under the dog, not set forward like a table. This asks for a long upper arm and a dog with correct angulation of shoulder will show forechest. Ideally,

Ch. Wrencliff Flying Scotsman of Winuwuk (ten CCs). Working Group winner.

Ch. Norwatch Brock Buster (twenty-nine CCs). Top Boxer UK (1982 and 1983). Sire of three UK Champions.

the foreleg extended upwards would bisect the shoulder-blade. I say, ideally, because the only shoulder assembly that meets the ideal is the Dachshund and we would not like our Boxers to have forehands like Dachshunds. Any problems in shoulder angulations, such as an upright shoulder, will result in short shoulder-blades and upper arms, which in turn results in short muscles causing the dog to be heavy in the shoulder (when you look at the dog from the front, you do not see smooth musculation over the shoulder but heavy bunchy musculation, a sure indication of a shoulder fault). Again, looking from the front, the front legs should be parallel. The Boxer is a square dog, the length of the body should equal the height at withers and the foreleg should be half the height of the body.

Feet

Feet should be like a cat's, with arched toes and good pads; the pasterns should be slightly slanted from the vertical, that is, the feet should be slightly in front of the foreleg.

Body

Ribs should be well sprung. The dog needs heart room for endurance and also to meet the demands of bursts of vigorous activity. The whole back should be broad with a firm topline and high tail set, the late Dibbie Somerfield of the Panfield prefix used to say that you should be able to stand a cup of tea on a Boxer's back! The Standard asks for a sloping back. This depends upon how you stand the dog: pulling the hindquarters back will lower the dog's rear and give him a sloping topline, which may be why some photographs show rather exaggerated poses. Personally, I think the Boxer should look like a dog rather than a hybrid hyena. Rib-cage should be long and the loin short; any problem here can show up in a soft topline. The chest or brisket should be deep and reach the elbows and the underline should show a graceful curve up from the chest to the loin. The Boxer should never be wasp-waisted. The underline used to be known as the line of beauty and the correct gentle curve gives a lot of class when looking at the dog's profile.

Ch. Starmark Sweet Talking Guy (twenty-four CCs). Sire of five UK Champions.

Ch. Marbelton Dressed to Kill (twenty-six CCs). Six times Working Group winner, twice Reserve Best in Show at All-Breed Championship Shows and twice British Boxer Club Champion of Champions.

Hindquarters

The hindquarters supply propulsion. The Boxer is a galloping dog and traditionally attacks by jumping at its target, so a very powerful rear end is required. We do not see many really poor backends in the modern Boxer; straight, or rear ends lacking angulation were far more prevalent in past years. What we want to see are broad thighs, with a graceful curve to the hock joint. When the dog is set up, it is normal to set the pasterns vertically and when set up in this way the stifle, or knee joint, should be directly under the hip, or ischial, protuberance. In plainer English, the hindquarters seen from the side should show a curve rearwards with the knee joint under the end of the bone that sticks out under the tail, we really want the hocks to be low to the ground rather than high. The Standard states that the leg from hock joint to foot is not quite vertical. This, of course, depends

62

Int. Ch. Milans Fashion Hint. One of the top producers ever, having sired sixty-five American Champions.

on how the dog is standing. When the dog is leaning forward or is set up with his rear end too far back, a variation from the vertical is far more pronounced.

When looking at the dog from the rear, the quarters should form a straight line from hip to foot, the angle between the legs varies depending on how the dog is standing. Some handlers set the dog up with rear feet well apart to give a sloping top line (the same effect will occur if the dog is straining at the lead). This is one of the problems associated with judging animals: quoting degrees and angles does not help because it all depends on how the dog is standing at that precise time. The Boxer should have a broad pelvis and well-developed hams. Remember, this is the driving unit and a weak rear is a major fault in a working dog.

Int. Ch. Scher-Khouns Meshack, sire of seventeen Champions.

General

The Boxer should have no loose skin. This is a common requirement for a fighting dog as it gives less opportunity for the opponent to grip; cropping and docking originated for similar reasons. Colour is basically cosmetic although a white Boxer is handicapped as a guard or war dog because it can be seen too easily. Black dogs are not acceptable; this is said to be due to an original breeder who specialized in black Boxers being a very unpopular person. Some colour combinations such as flashy, dark brindles and deer-red fawns are quite spectacular but should never be favoured above plainer but more typical animals.

This chapter covers the development of the Standard, the initial reasons for the specific points of the breed and the changes caused by the change from bull-baiter to companion dog. It is also possible to understand why top quality Boxers are not easy to breed with his most distinctive head that defies nature and the perfection required in his body and construction. The Standard can easily be learned by heart but the only true way to understand the breed is to study top specimens. It is the same as in other professions: you can learn the theory but you need a few years practical experience to understand the subject fully.

5

Getting Started

Having made the decision to acquire a good Boxer puppy, you will now need to ensure that the puppy you choose is of sound mind and body. I hope that this chapter will give the first-time buyer some hints to bring the search for a good puppy to a successful conclusion, irrespective of whether you are looking for a potential show prospect or a good companion.

When we started in our lovely breed thirty years ago, we certainly did not foresee that a large portion of our lives would eventually be dedicated to showing. We did what many other Boxer beginners do: we contacted a well-known kennel and asked for a fawn, male dog – for a pet. The puppy duly arrived and we thought he was a super specimen. I can clearly remember clutching the Breed Standard in one hand and going over the dog with the other. As we checked the dog point by point, our conviction that we had a certain champion grew. What we did not realize was that we were fitting the Standard to the dog and not checking the dog to the Standard.

The first show was looked forward to with great excitement and was followed by a massive anticlimax. The judge was exceedingly kind and showed us where the dog failed as a show specimen. Of course, the breeder had sold us exactly what we had asked for: a sound male dog with a super temperament of pet, not show, quality. He lived with us for many years and was a delight to own.

However, the show bug had really bitten us so we decided to get a good show bitch. We contacted the breeder of our pet dog and asked her for a show-quality female. Again, we got exactly what we had specified – a pretty, brindle bitch of show quality. She gave us great pleasure in the show ring but unfortunately, she died at eighteen months old. Having tasted some success, we went on to acquire two more bitches of show quality. One won our first Challenge Certificate and the other produced the first Champion we had bred. All this took place in the mid 1950s, and was the start of our kennels.

The first thing we did correctly was to go to a breeder and state our requirements. Before making an investment in a puppy, you must decide exactly what you want: a show or pet dog, male or female, fawn or brindle. When you have that clear in your mind, you are half-way there.

The main difference between a pet and show puppy are quality and price: the higher the quality, the higher the price. There are fewer top-quality puppies possessing the attributes that lead to a future as a show winner and these differences are probably not even distinguishable to the untrained eye. Really good puppies are few in number so that the law of supply and demand operates. Actually, the basic costs of mating the bitch, rearing the puppies and any vet's fees are applicable to any puppy so the cost differential between puppies may not be so great as anticipated, when the difference in cost is spread over the life span of the average Boxer the extra expense incurred by buying a quality puppy is nominal.

Before deciding between a male or female puppy, it is important to know whether you intend to show and breed or whether you just want a companion dog.

I would advise anyone who intends to breed to start with a bitch puppy. A good well-bred bitch can still produce excellent puppies if mated to the right sire, even if she herself loses some of her show quality as she develops (as often happens with bitches). It is possible to purchase a good dog puppy that can develop into a top-class specimen that other people would use as a stud. However, the odds are stacked against you as no breeder would ever want to part with a potential Champion male; we did at one time and I have regretted it ever since.

If you are looking for a companion, it does not really matter whether you decide on a dog or a bitch; both will give devotion and will protect you and your family. You will have the problem of a bitch coming into season twice a year but they are generally less aggressive towards other dogs than their male counterparts. We must also remember that dogs are ready to mate at any time and an over-sexed dog can be a nuisance and a real embarrassment when some-one who is not dog-minded visits.

The base colour is mainly personal preference: some people like fawns, others like brindles. There seems to be a preponderance of brindles at the time of writing because most of the top studs are brindles. If you are looking for a show dog, you will probably be offered a puppy with white markings; these can be very attractive and eyecatching if they are confined to the right areas. However, one thing is important: an all-white or nearly all-white Boxer has no chance in the show ring. They can be registered at the UK Kennel Club but most breeders will not breed from a white Boxer. I have heard of cases where Boxers have been sold to unwary customers as a unique and desirable animal; do not be taken in, these can only be considered as pets and nothing more.

Having decided what sort of puppy would suit you, you should approach a reputable breeder to see if a puppy is available. A good breeder has a reputation to protect and will certainly try hard to meet your requirements especially if you are looking for a show animal: sooner or later it will appear in the show ring and no breeder wants to see a poor specimen carrying his or her prefix in full view of the public.

My suggestion would be to visit some shows that only feature Boxers. These are known as Boxer Breed or Speciality Shows depending on the country where they are being held. In the UK you would look for a Breed Show. The dates and venues appear in the weekly dog periodicals. Alternatively, ask your local breed club or write to the Kennel Club who will assist you.

When you arrive at the show, buy a catalogue listing the classes, the exhibits' names, the names of the exhibitors and the breeders of the exhibits. The names of the exhibits will include the kennel prefix or affix, which will identify the breeder. For example, my kennel prefix is Winuwuk: all the dogs I breed or register have Winuwuk in their names. The Seefeld prefix identifies Mrs Heath as the breeder, and so on. When you see dogs consistently winning from a kennel, and even more important, consistently winning for other owners, put that kennel on your list of possibilities. You can now contact the breeders and state what you are looking for, making it perfectly clear what you require: male or female, show or companion and colour preference. The breeder will let you know what puppies are available. You may have to go on a waiting list because there is quite a demand for quality puppies from premier kennels. Some puppies in a litter will not be quite up to show standard, although this may only be apparent to the experienced eye. These make very good companion dogs.

You may have heard that pedigree dogs, and especially show dogs, are so highly bred that they are neurotic, unstable and more prone to illness than cross-bred dogs. This is a fallacy. Show dogs are handled by judges who make quite an intimate examination of them, including an inspection of the mouth and teeth. They must have an equable temperament so that they are not upset by travelling long distances to shows and sittting on show benches during judging; they have to show in the close confines of the show ring with, perhaps, twenty other dogs present and any display of aggression is frowned upon; aggression towards the judge is grounds for disqualification.

Any breeder who breeds from unsound stock, that is, not sound in body and mind, is wasting time and money and will see the end of all hope and aspirations in a very short time. Some people who have come to us for a puppy have been quite shocked to find common ancestors in the pedigree. We all have an in-built aversion to the principle of mating close relatives. However, a clever breeder will use close breeding to obtain the virtues without doubling up on faults. Agreed, in-breeding can be dangerous unless the breeder knows the background of the breeding stock but when utilized by an expert it can offer a short cut to achieving quality stock at the start of a breeding programme. This subject is covered more fully in the chapter on breeding (*see* pages 72–78).

My main reason for suggesting you go to a reputable breeder is that you can expect to buy a well-bred puppy, expertly reared and properly cared for, which means that you are off to a good start. Puppies with a lot of potential can go wrong but a poor puppy has no potential at all. Picking puppies as potential show winners does require expertise and experience so I would suggest that you allow the breeder to assess the quality of the puppy and rely on the honesty and integrity of the breeder; most breeders are careful of their reputation and will ensure that you get exactly what you ask for. More information on picking puppies when you have bred your first litter is given in Chapter 10 (*see* page 109).

There are some points you should look for that can help you even if you are an absolute beginner. It always helps to see the sire and dam if possible. I say if possible because you may be offered the pick of a litter by the breeder's stud dog, out of a bitch from another kennel or the puppy may be out of the breeder's bitch by an outside stud dog. If you can see the parents or one parent, see if the animal appeals to you, is in good condition and has a happy temperament. There is a good chance that the puppy will show similar characteristics.

Have a look at the litter, which is probably around seven weeks old. That quiet puppy may look sweet and tug at your heart strings but it may be sickly or grow up too much of an introvert for the show ring and is more suitable for a companion dog. Check that the puppies are well cared for, clean and with no signs of skin problems. Pick

This is the temperament to look for in a show puppy.

it up and check the muscle tone: it should feel strong and active – a limp puppy spells problems. A healthy puppy has a distinctive odour and will smell clean and sweet. The eyes should be clear of discharge and dark blue in colour, a light shade of blue could result in a light eye in later life – a problem with a show animal but not so important in a pet. The third eyelid should show a dark rim. The puppy's skin should be loose and very often shows wrinkles on the body, and the whole puppy should be plump and sturdy. Male dogs should show signs that his testicles are either down or on their way down towards the scrotum. The scrotum itself is not fully developed at this age and in some lines the testicles descend later than in other lines but it is reassuring to see something on its way.

You can see what colour the puppy will be, either fawn of a varying degree of richness, or brindle. A show puppy will most likely show some attractive white markings. It is not easy to win without these markings in some countries although the Standard states that white markings are acceptable not mandatory.

When checking the puppy do not make a great display of it. Dog breeders are proud people so show a little sensitivity and tact.

It is not feasible to give guide-lines on how much you should pay for a puppy. The cost varies from country to country, area to area and even kennel to kennel. The basic rule is that the higher the potential of the puppy, the higher the price. As good puppies are always wanted, the law of supply and demand operates and so you must expect to pay a reasonable price. There are many hidden costs in breeding a litter: the initial cost of the dam, the stud fee, any travelling expenses, rearing and feeding the litter and any veterinary expenses. Most breeders do not take their time into account – if they did, prices would soar. From the breeder's viewpoint, if the prospective owners cannot afford to pay a fair price for the puppy, they may not be able to afford to keep it. There are too many dogs thrown out because their owners have underestimated the cost of keeping a dog in good condition.

You can reduce your outlay by buying a puppy on breeding terms. This means that you pay a reduced price but are committed to giving the breeder a choice of puppies from the first and perhaps other litters. You will usually find that the breeder will retain the right to nominate the stud dog to be used.

If you are buying a dog, the agreement usually allows the breeder a number of free services or a share in the stud fees. Be sure that an agreement of this type is fair to both parties, is clearly understood and is laid down in writing and signed by both parties. It is possible to acquire a super bitch of good type and excellent breeding at reduced cost if she does not have the fashionable white markings. She may not be the great winner you are looking for but mated to the right dog could produce puppies of the highest quality. It is not easy to win with a plain bitch (although there is no reason why you should not) so you may have to wait a couple of years until she has produced suitable puppies before you can enter into serious competition.

6

Breeding

If you have a well-bred bitch who has been reared properly and, possibly, been shown with some success, you may feel that you would like to breed a litter from her. The first and, perhaps, the most important question you need to ask yourself is why you wish to breed puppies. If your reason is purely to make some money, forget it right now. The Boxer and Dog Rescue Kennels are full of discarded puppies and older dogs that were produced for purely commercial reasons. Many show kennels seem to think that they should have the monopoly of puppy production but there is no reason why a reputable breeder should not produce quality puppies for sale as companions. The important thing is to produce puppies that are sound and of high quality, and the aim should always be to improve your stock. The perfect Boxer has never been bred and probably never will be; one of the main fascinations of breeding is its pursuit of the impossible. Our best Boxer Champion had at least two areas that could be improved but we have not even bred another who is as good, let alone better, but we will keep on trying!

To make improvements in future generations we must first attack the problems. The principle that once a problem has been defined, the solution is simple, can be applied to your breeding programme: you must know the faults in your stock before you can make improvements. Take off your rose-tinted spectacles, take a long, hard look at your bitch, take note of her faults and you are starting on the path to improvement.

Let us have a brief and rather superficial look at genetics. My simplistic approach to this complex subject will horrify the experts but will give you an idea of what genetics is about. If you want to learn more, there are many good books aimed at the dog breeder and students of the science.

We take for granted that if we mate a Boxer to a Boxer we will produce Boxers and not any other breed. Sometimes something unexpected crops up in the best of blood-lines. Why should this happen?

Until around 1900, even biologists could not give the answers, although Gregor Mendel had carried out research into the inheritance of characteristics some forty years earlier. The rediscovery of Mendel's experiment on garden peas gave impetus to the research that led to the modern science of genetics. Before the mode of inheritance was understood, people thought that the blood somehow mixed and was diluted down through successive generations. So how are inherited characteristics handed on? What decides that the union of a sperm and an ovum will result in a Boxer and not a Great Dane or a Boston Terrier?

An important basic discovery was the isolation of a vast number of discrete characteristics that combine to distinguish a particular animal. These characteristics are called genes, and are the coded instructions that are responsible for deciding the finished animal – in this case, our Boxer. It was also discovered that the genes specifying an individual characteristic and the way they are handed on to future generations follow a relatively simple law. Because the same laws apply to all living creatures, the effects of inheritance can be studied using creatures of a short life span, such as mice and even fruit flies, so reducing the research time. The results can then be applied to animals of longer life spans, including dogs.

In basic terms, a dog has a pair of genes for each trait but only one of these is passed on to his offspring; so, the single genes from the sire and dam form the pair of genes in the offspring. Another important point is that an individual gene can be dominant or recessive: the dominant gene will, as the name implies, take precedence over the recessive gene although the recessive gene is still present and can show effect in certain circumstances. For example, let us look at something we can all see: coat colour. The diagrams on page 74 show how the laws of inheritance determine whether the coat will be brindle or fawn. Capitals are used for dominant genes and lower case for recessive genes; brindle is defined by 'B' and fawn by 'f'. We can now say that brindle coats are dominant over fawns. In this case, all four puppies will be brindle, each puppy having inherited a dominant brindle gene from its sire. If we mate two of these puppies together, the resulting litter will consist of three brindles and one fawn. The diagrams illustrate that each parent has two genes for any trait and passes one on to his offspring (the other being supplied by the other parent). If a puppy inherits identical genes from both parents, the dog is termed homozygous for that characteristic and if they are dissimilar it is said to be heterozygous. However, even if a dog has hetero-

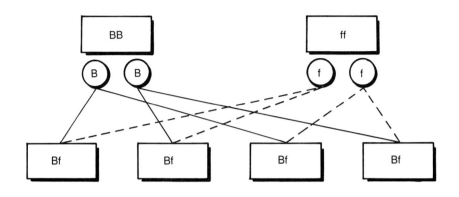

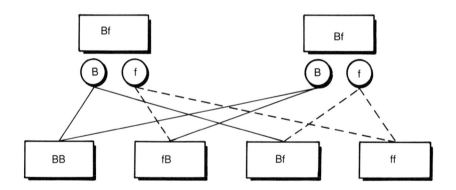

Simple inheritance charts.

zygous traits, he will still carry the recessive gene. This recessive gene can be passed on until it meets a matching recessive gene; it then reappears for good or bad.

The animal's actual physical makeup is called the phenotype; its genetic makeup is called its genotype. A moment's thought and it is possible to understand that a dog may not produce his own physical characteristics but those dictated by his genotype. We can also gather that show wins are a result of the phenotype but a stud career is based on genotype. This explains the old saying, 'the only thing that makes a good sire is the quality of his get.' The top-winning males obviously get more good bitches to them and have a better chance to show their qualities as a sire. I wonder how many potential super studs have spent their lives sleeping on the couch in the sitting room! One successful sire only got his first chance because although his owner had booked another dog, a heavy storm made travelling impossible: the owner used her own dog and another good stud dog was discovered.

However, for a male to be truly dominant, that is, pass on his own excellence, he must be genetically dominant in these traits. If a poor dog passes on traits better than he possesses himself, he must be recessive in these traits so we prefer to use a dominant sire. A prepotent dog is one who stamps his type on his offspring. If we are considering an excellent show/stud dog we are really saying that his phenotype and genotype are similar; the important point is that the dog possesses many pure and desirable dominant traits. The best way to fix these traits is by close breeding, that is, line- or in-breeding. Many of the dominant sires show this type of breeding. Red Baron's breeding (*see* page 76) is an example. The benefit of in-breeding is not only that it can result in a dog dominant in the traits that you want; it can also throw up any problems lurking in the background in recessive genes.

Most breeders want to establish a line, that is a family of better-than-average dogs who tend to show the same characteristics. This sort of line can only be established by careful line-breeding. Once you have developed a string of your own, your litters will show a general rise in quality and you can keep yourself in show stock without having to breed dozens of puppies. Many people run successful show kennels by breeding like-to-like; this can result in high-quality stock but you cannot really be sure of the genotype. Most of us cannot afford to keep too many dogs so we attempt this search for excellence through line-breeding.

The conclusion to be drawn is that although it is not necessary to be a geneticist to breed good dogs, many people have unknowingly used genetic principles over the years by trial and error, experience and simple common sense.

For your first litter, you could start by asking your bitch's breeder who would be a suitable sire. If your bitch is line-bred, this is usually a sign of long-term planning and you could be taking advantage of years of experience by following the breeder's suggestion. Alternatively, take notice of the current successful show dogs and see

Parents	Grandparents	GG-parents	GGG-parents
		Ch. Milan's Fashion Hint	Ch. Salgray's Fashion Plate
			Ch.Gaymitz Jet Action
	Ch. Scher Khoun's Shadrack		
		Ch. Scher Khoun's Carousel	Ch. Standfast of Blossomlea
Sire Ch. Scher Khoun's Abednego			Ch. Scher Khoun's Apricot Brandy
		Ch. Standfast of Blossomlea	Ruda River's Happy Go Lucky
	Ch. Scher Khoun's Carousel		Ch. Fireside Chat of Blossomlea
		Ch. Scher Khoun's Apricot Bandy	Ch. Standfast of Blossomlea
			Ch. Scher Khoun's Fire Imp
		Ch. Scher Khoun's Meshack	Ch. Scher Khoun's Shadrack
			Ch. Scher Khoun's Syncopation
	Ch. Holly Lane's Winter Forecast		
		Ch. Holly Lane's Windstorm	Ch. Brayshaw's Masquerader
Dam Milray's Flame of Candelwood			Ch. Holly Lane's Cookie
		Ch. Pinebrook's Radiation	Candelwood's Straight Shot
	Candelwood's Cinderella		Oliver's Happy Talk
		Candelwood's Cassandra	Ch. Treceder's Shine Boy
			Candelwood's Gina

Note: Abednego from a mother/son mating. Meshack from a brother/sister mating. Meshack sired seventeen American Champions; Shadrack sired thirty-nine American Champions; Fashion Hint sired sixty-five American Champions; and Fashion Plate sired sixty-three American Champions.

Pedigree of Winuwuk Milray's Red Baron of Valvay, imported to Britain from USA.

Ch. Seefeld Picasso (twenty-four CCs). Best in Show, twice Reserve Best in Show and five times Working Group winner. Sire of fifty-eight Champions worldwide and eighteen UK Champions. Top British sire.

what sire is consistently producing winners and stamping quality on his offspring. You have studied your bitch and decided what her good points are and where she fails. If you are an ardent student of the Boxer you will also know where her breeding shows strengths and weaknesses. What you are looking for is a dog who consistently produces the traits that are lacking in your bitch. For instance, if your bitch has a weak muzzle, you should ensure that the stud dog does not possess a similar weakness in his breeding. In this way, you can make practical use of genetics. You can now decide to line-breed to establish your particular line or you can do as many successful people do: mate good producing sires to good quality bitches, always being careful to double up on virtues and to avoid doubling up on faults. Be very careful if you use an outcross (a sire from another line

Ch. Tyegarth Famous Grouse, dominant UK sire of the late 1980s.

of breeding) because you may be introducing a problem that could be very difficult to eradicate – this is why many established kennels tend to use dogs from within their own strain.

What is the penalty of very close in-breeding? We have found that the first thing we lose is substance, so an outcross is needed sooner or later to bring in some hybrid vigour – this normally brings back size and substance straight away. If you have a small Boxer, do not over respond and mate it to a real monster, you could end up with a mixture of small puppies and huge puppies. The correct way is to breed to dogs of the right size and the same reasoning goes for any other point that needs improving. Another old fable is that if a bitch is mated by a dog of another breed or a cross-breed, she is somehow ruined for future breeding. Simple genetics show that this is impossible – each litter is a closed event.

Your bitch will be approaching her second or third season, and at least eighteen months old, when you decide to mate her. The first thing to notice is when she starts to show colour, i.e. bleed from the vulva. At this point, contact the owner of the stud dog you have

Back in Town's son, Rainey Lanes Grand Slam who sired nineteen Champions.

Norwatch Mustang Wine. Top dam UK; dam of five Champions who have won fifty-seven CCs. Six times winner of British Boxer Club Dam of Merit title.

selected and book the service. Next, you have to decide when she is ready for mating. There are several indicators. For the inexperienced, it is wisest to watch for the colour of discharge from the vulva to change to a paler shade. If the discharge is bright red, it is too early for her to be covered. The more experienced breeder can also get an indication from the condition of the vulva, which tends to tighten up a little. The sure indication is when she 'stands' to a dog, that is presents her rear end and holds her tail to one side – a stance which is difficult to describe but unmistakable; she will also stand if you pass your hand along her spine. At this sign, you can be sure she is ready, and can take her to the sire, having warned his owner that you are on your way. Normally, a bitch is ready twelve days from the day she first shows colour but some bitches are ready early or late in their season so it is still advisable to look out for the signs.

80

If you have left it too late, you will have to forget about having a litter until the next season. If you are too early, the bitch will let you know that she is not ready and an experienced stud dog will be half-hearted about the whole affair. The usual cause of missing the right time is the owners bringing the bitch at a time that suits them and not the bitch – it is amazing how most bitches arrive at the weekend and how upset the owners are when they are told that they are too early or too late. Of course, if you own the sire yourself, you can try them to see when she is ready. Do not forget to exercise her before the mating and make sure she has relieved herself.

You should have made your arrangements over stud fees at the time of booking. Any special arrangements should be agreed and understood before the mating. For instance, the sire's owner may wish to take a puppy instead of a stud fee. Such an arrangement is common where the bitch is considered to be of good breeding and high quality. Make sure you are agreed on the puppy you have to return to the sire's owner: the pick or second pick of the litter, or whatever. It should be remembered that the owner may have turned down an alternative bitch in order to accommodate you, and is taking the risk that your bitch will not miss (especially if she has not had a previous litter) so do not complain if you have a small litter or the sire owner's choice is the puppy you have set your heart on – that is the risk you are taking. Finally, make sure that all required documentation is completed, certificate of mating, etc., according to your particular Kennel Club's rules, and do not forget that you need a copy of the sire's pedigree and registration number.

7

Mating

When your bitch shows signs that she is ready for mating, inform the stud dog owner and arrange your time of arrival. I always aim to arrive early enough to exercise my Boxer and let her relieve herself. Kennel owners are busy people, so this should not be treated as a social outing for bringing the whole family along to: two people are much more welcome than seven. Many kennels are in rural areas and surrounded by land so it is important to make your presence known before you bring your bitch in from the car – it is not a good start to have to fight off a couple of amorous males while trying to ring the doorbell.

The stud's owner will control the mating. Listen closely to what you are told and follow the instructions you are given. There are different approaches to mating and we like it to be as natural as possible. We put a stout collar on the bitch so that the owner can grasp both sides of the collar at the sides of the neck and use the forearms to keep the bitch's head looking forward so that she cannot turn her head and have a nip at the dog. We introduce the dog to the bitch while they are both on leads. We find that if the bitch is ready she will flirt with the dog and we let them both off the lead to allow the dog to court her. A maiden bitch, one who has not been mated before, can be very coy and it is amusing to see how a dog will court her and persuade her to be receptive.

Before mating begins, it is important for the dogs to be in a quiet place. If the floor is not non-slip, mats should be laid down to prevent the dog's feet from slipping. Once the bitch stands for the dog, we ask the bitch's owner to hold her head in the way described. The dog will clasp the bitch with his forelegs and start to mate her, at which point, his handler will control the dog and make any small adjustments required to help him penetrate. When the dog penetrates he will thrust for a short time before becoming passive and just holding the bitch. The dog's handler will turn the dog and they will tie: this is when the bulb at the base of the penis expands, locking him into the bitch. On average, this tie lasts for twenty minutes but the time varies – the longest tie I have witnessed lasted two and a half hours. We always have a couple of low stools handy so we can at least sit down while waiting for the dogs to part. When the dogs do part, take your bitch away and let her relax.

A maiden bitch can be unpredictable; she may stand well but then get excited and try and break away from the dog. Remember, it is your job to control her. We have mated many bitches this way without ever having the dog bitten – an experienced sire is pretty bright and seems to sense when the bitch is going to snap at him. Boxer bitches give very little trouble if they are ready and can usually be handled by a stranger. We have found that a troublesome bitch can be very good if her owner is not present at the mating and we often handle her ourselves without any problems although we do like the owners to see the tie, just to reassure them that she has been mated to the right dog – this avoids any doubt or argument later on.

We have found that the usual cause of the bitch getting upset during the courting phase is that it is too early in her cycle and very often, she gives no trouble when mated one or two days later. We have found that this method of waiting for the bitch to be ready may take a little more time but we never have to resort to muzzling or forced matings.

You will have noticed that handling the bitch is quite a passive role; when you are handling the sire you have to be more active. Starting a young dog off in stud work can require a lot of patience. A potential sire should commence his stud career with an experienced and steady bitch – a maiden pair can really compound the problem. It may seem strange that dogs should get problems in carrying out a perfectly normal function but conditions are rather different to a totally natural mating. We like to get the dog used to being helped if necessary and accept being handled.

We normally start a young dog off at about fourteen months old, introducing him to an experienced bitch who stands like a rock. At this age they are full of enthusiasm but have little sense of direction so you need to keep his attention concentrated at the right end of the bitch. When he finally clasps the bitch you may find that he is still in the wrong place. We find that the best way to help him is to kneel at one side of the bitch (her right side if you are right-handed) and put your arm from the side down under her stomach until your hand is between her legs. Put a finger each side of her vulva and gently move her until the dog can penetrate. It is easier than it sounds. You may find that the dog is tiring himself and becoming rather half-hearted, in which case, take him away from the bitch and give him a rest and a little water before bringing him back to start again.

With some dogs, it does need a lot of patience; others get the idea quite quickly. Never get annoyed or you will destroy the dog's confidence. Tell him he is a good boy and give him lots of encouragement. Sooner or later, he will manage to penetrate and will go into the active, thrusting phase; you can then move to his side. Following the active part of the mating, he will be quite passive but still clasp the bitch with his forelegs. At this point, you have to turn him. Give him a few minutes until he starts to become uneasy, and loosens his clasp on the bitch; very often, he will start lifting one of his hind legs. Some dogs will actually turn themselves but we usually take his hind leg, pass it gently over the bitch's back until the dog and the bitch are standing back to back. This is the tie, when the dog cannot withdraw from the bitch. Do not try and part them – you can seriously harm both of them. We pass a scarf around the upper part of the dog's and the bitch's hindquarters to hold them firmly together.

After a while, the dog will start looking towards his rear when you should gently check to see if they are still tied. When the tie breaks, the dog will drop out of the bitch and you can take the bitch away. Remove the dog so that he can clean himself up; the penis will be distended and will look quite messy. Everything returns to normal quite rapidly but just keep an eye on him to make sure that the penis does return to its sheath. If it does not, gently try to ease the sheath over the penis. Do not use brute force: if you still have a problem take him to your veterinary surgeon who will carry out the manipulation required. We have not found this to be a common problem – of the many stud dogs we have owned, only one has ever experienced it.

With maiden bitches, problems are usually caused by the bitch not standing properly and tucking her vulva underneath her so that the dog cannot mate her. With your arm and hand, adjust the bitch and lift her rear until the dog can penetrate. A maiden can resent being mated and may try to throw the dog off; this is where the bitch's handler controls her by gripping the collar and holding her forehand down so that she cannot rear up. She may also show signs of discomfort when the active phase of the mating is over and the dog is passive, still clasping her but putting his full weight on her, so keep control during this time. The dogs usually settle down once the sire has turned although they can get bored and try to walk away from each other. The scarf around their hindquarters will prevent this.

84

We are often asked if a successful mating should be repeated. Our experience indicates that it should!

Some dogs take longer to tie than others. We had one male who we thought did not tie until we discovered that we were turning him too quickly. Another cause of not achieving a tie is that the bitch is a little early in her cycle. I have made many attempts to find out why dogs are different to other domestic animals in this peculiar mating procedure but have never found a definitive answer. We did have a Boston Terrier who never tied, though he was a very virile sire. However, we do like to see a tie because you get the feeling that at least the mechanics have been performed as expected.

If you have a slow dog, that is, one who seems to treat the mating procedure as something rather distasteful, we find that making a fuss of the bitch and raking her back with your fingers sometimes arouses interest; also, lifting her up by the forelegs will often trigger a response in the dog. However, a good stud should have a strong sexual drive and I would be a little dubious about the real worth of a male who had little interest in the opposite sex, although he may be a late developer, or have a health problem which your vet could help with.

This all seems very complicated but it is a perfectly natural function that must be carried out in order to breed your lovely litter of puppies. Again, you can see the value of starting with a bitch: you will have some idea of the mating ritual by watching an experienced handler at work before you try and handle your own stud dog.

Most matings take place with very little trouble. It is the owners who are affected more often than the bitch. We have had people burst into tears while their pride and joy is being deflowered so we always keep aspirin, handkerchiefs and a pot of tea brewing. One male owner was very annoyed that his bitch appeared to enjoy the experience. Mating can be a worrying thing for the novice owner but it is a very natural function and perfectly normal procedure to a breeder.

It is worth remembering that you have a short-coated dog of good size – in comparison to many breeds, Boxers are easy!

8

Pregnancy and Whelping

After the mating, we have to wait to see if the bitch is in whelp – a period that requires patience. The time from mating to whelping is normally about sixty-three days. Around the fifth week of pregnancy, your bitch will start to look a little plump, this is more obvious following a meal. There are other signs of pregnancy to be noticed: the vulva never seems to reduce to its original size and the nipples become more prominent although the most reliable sign is an obvious increase in size. Waiting for this confirmation can be an anxious time and there is a temptation to get a professional opinion but by the time her pregnancy can be confirmed it is usually obvious that she is in whelp. I do not like to see the bitch appear to be in whelp too early as this usually signifies a false pregnancy and the bitch can deflate as fast as she inflates.

After mating, feed and exercise your bitch quite normally – you do not want the prospective mother to become too fat. In the fourth week of pregnancy, you can start adding some calcium and extra vitamins to her diet. Any reputable additives will suffice but always follow the instructions and do not add a little bit extra for luck. It is always tempting to draw up a diet sheet but bitches are very individual. You cannot feed according to the size of the litter as, obviously, you do not know how many puppies she is carrying. You really need to ensure that the bitch has enough biscuit and meat to keep her well covered without being gross. We increase the meat more than biscuit in order to cope with the increased appetite and give milk and cod liver oil instead of additives. Plenty of fresh drinking water should always be available, especially at the later stages of pregnancy when a bitch seems to have a bottomless thirst.

The aim is to ensure the bitch has enough protein and calcium to build up strong whelps without getting so fat and soft in condition that you get into whelping problems. Your bitch should have been in top condition and wormed before you mated her but if you see that she has passed worms or you suspect she has worms, it is possible to

Puppies are due on the sixty-third day. The bitch has made her nest. Whelping usually takes place at night.

worm her during her pregnancy. However, talk to your veterinary before taking action.

Exercise normally until she starts slowing up. If she normally runs with other dogs, I would be careful of any rough play, she does not want any rough and tumble games. In the last weeks of pregnancy, the bitch really fills up and the pups appear to move back or drop. When the bitch is resting, you can see the pups move about, lumps appearing and disappearing often to the future mum's astonishment. The time quoted for the gestation period of the dog is sixty-three days, although we usually find our bitches tend to whelp a day or two early, sometimes a day or two late, but very rarely on the sixty-third day! However, the gestation table on page 89 is a useful guide to the probable day of whelping.

You can tell if your bitch is approaching the actual whelping phase by quite noticable changes in behaviour: turning up her nose at her food; getting into a quiet corner away from people; and starting to make a nest by scratching her bed up are all positive signs. When she starts to pant and look generally uneasy, it is a pretty solid indication

Gestation table. First column of each pair lists the mating date; second column lists the whelping date.

Jan	Mar	Feb	Apr	Mar	May	Apr	June	May	July	June	Aug	July	Sept	Aug	Oct	Sept	Nov	Oct	Dec	Nov	Jan	Dec	Feb
1	5	1	5	1	3	1	3	1	3	1	3	1	2	1	3	1	3	1	3	1	3	1	2
2	6	2	6	2	4	2	4	2	4	2	4	2	3	2	4	2	4	2	4	2	4	2	3
3	7	3	7	3	5	3	5	3	5	3	5	3	4	3	5	3	5	3	5	3	5	3	4
4	8	4	8	4	6	4	6	4	6	4	6	4	5	4	6	4	6	4	6	4	6	4	5
5	9	5	9	5	7	5	7	5	7	5	7	5	6	5	7	5	7	5	7	5	7	5	6
6	10	6	10	6	8	6	8	6	8	6	8	6	7	6	8	6	8	6	8	6	8	6	7
7	11	7	11	7	9	7	9	7	9	7	9	7	8	7	9	7	9	7	9	7	9	7	8
8	12	8	12	8	10	8	10	8	10	8	10	8	9	8	10	8	10	8	10	8	10	8	9
9	13	9	13	9	11	9	11	9	11	9	11	9	10	9	11	9	11	9	11	9	11	9	10
10	14	10	14	10	12	10	12	10	12	10	12	10	11	10	12	10	12	10	12	10	12	10	11
11	15	11	15	11	13	11	13	11	13	11	13	11	12	11	13	11	13	11	13	11	13	11	12
12	16	12	16	12	14	12	14	12	14	12	14	12	13	12	14	12	14	12	14	12	14	12	13
13	17	13	17	13	15	13	15	13	15	13	15	13	14	13	15	13	15	13	15	13	15	13	14
14	18	14	18	14	16	14	16	14	16	14	16	14	15	14	16	14	16	14	16	14	16	14	15
15	19	15	19	15	17	15	17	15	17	15	17	15	16	15	17	15	17	15	17	15	17	15	16
16	20	16	20	16	18	16	18	16	18	16	18	16	17	16	18	16	18	16	18	16	18	16	17
17	21	17	21	17	19	17	19	17	19	17	19	17	18	17	19	17	19	17	19	17	19	17	18
18	22	18	22	18	20	18	20	18	20	18	20	18	19	18	20	18	20	18	20	18	20	18	19
19	23	19	23	19	21	19	21	19	21	19	21	19	20	19	21	19	21	19	21	19	21	19	20
20	24	20	24	20	22	20	22	20	22	20	22	20	21	20	22	20	22	20	22	20	22	20	21
21	25	21	25	21	23	21	23	21	23	21	23	21	22	21	23	21	23	21	23	21	23	21	22
22	26	22	26	22	24	22	24	22	24	22	24	22	23	22	24	22	24	22	24	22	24	22	23
23	27	23	27	23	25	23	25	23	25	23	25	23	24	23	25	23	25	23	25	23	25	23	24
24	28	24	28	24	26	24	26	24	26	24	26	24	25	24	26	24	26	24	26	24	26	24	25
25	29	25	29	25	27	25	27	25	27	25	27	25	26	25	27	25	27	25	27	25	27	25	26
26	30	26	30	26	28	26	28	26	28	26	28	26	27	26	28	26	28	26	28	26	28	26	27
27	31	27	May 1	27	29	27	29	27	29	27	29	27	28	27	29	27	29	27	29	27	29	27	28
28	Apr 1	28	May 2	28	30	28	30	28	30	28	30	28	29	28	30	28	30	28	30	28	30	28	Mar 1
29	Apr 2			29	31	29	July 1	29	31	29	31	29	30	29	31	29	Dec 1	29	31	29	31	29	Mar 2
30	Apr 3			30	June 1	30	July 2	30	Aug 1	30	Sept 1	30	Oct 1	30	Nov 1	30	Dec 2	30	Jan 1	30	Feb 1	30	Mar 3
31	Apr 4			31	June 2			31	Aug 2			31	Oct 2	31	Nov 2			31	Jan 2			31	Mar 4

Gestation table. First column lists mating date; second column lists whelping date.

The whelping box should be large enough for stretching out. Notice the rails round the side and the infra-red lamp for warmth.

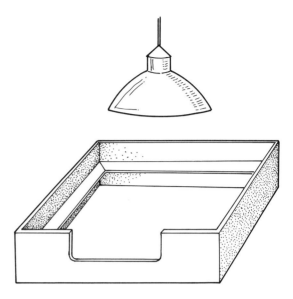

that things are starting to move. The clinical sign is her temperature dropping to 98 degrees and the pups usually arrive within 24 hours.

It is surprising how many bitches start to whelp on their owner's bed or in some other quite unsuitable place. This can be avoided by having a suitable whelping box ready in a quiet spot so that you can settle your bitch down in comfortable surroundings. A suitable box is shown in the above illustration. We always fit rails on the inside so that the puppies cannot get crushed between the bitch and the whelping box – an idea borrowed from pig breeders. The best place to whelp is in a warm outside shed or an unused room. The bitch does need to be undisturbed and she will not want to produce her puppies in front of an audience.

When your bitch starts showing signs that whelping is about to commence, lead her to the box and you will find she will settle down very quickly. Put some layers of clean newspaper in the box so she can have a really good scratch up and let her get on with the job. The room should be comfortably warm for the bitch and the new puppies and so we use an infra-red lamp hung over the whelping box to ensure there is heat where needed. Items you will need include cotton wool, sterile scissors (preferably blunt) and a rough towel.

When you introduce your bitch to the whelping box, she will probably be very restless, pant heavily and start puffing and blowing; she will also look at her rear as if expecting something to appear. Do not keep fussing and disturbing her; just keep a watch and make note of when the first labour contractions start. Labour always seems to start during the night. We have never had a bitch whelp during the day so be prepared for a night-time vigil. You need to keep a careful watch. Do not let your bitch strain so much that she exhausts herself. If she works hard for a period approaching two hours, call your veterinary surgeon. This is of paramount importance because your bitch may be in serious trouble. For instance, there may be a breeched puppy holding everything up and with problems such as these, your bitch will need professional help. The idea is to give the bitch a fair chance to whelp by herself but without allowing her to get so weak that she cannot stand surgical intervention if it becomes necessary. Specific whelping problems and emergencies will be dealt with in the section on complications (*see* pages 95–100).

Boxers are generally very straightforward in the whelping box so I shall continue to describe a natural whelping. The contractions will increase in frequency and become stronger. You will see the vulva

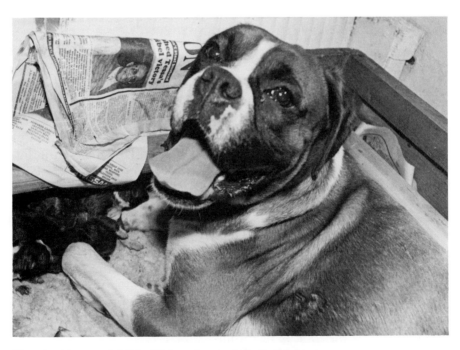

Do not get too worried if the bitch pants, especially if whelping in a heated room.

91

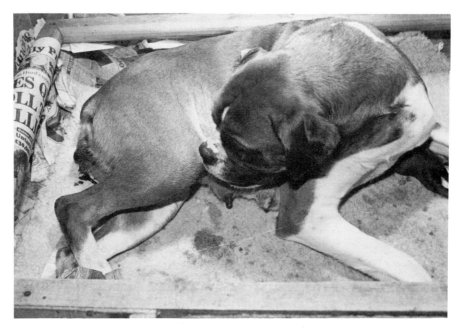

*The bitch usually indicates that another puppy is due by looking at
her rear end.*

enlarge and then a water bag protrude from it. A few more contractions and the puppy will slide out into the whelping box, neatly
enclosed in a transparent sac. Your bitch will immediately rip the sac
open and clean the puppy. Make sure that she bites through the
umbilical cord; most bitches have no problem with this but if she
cannot manage, use your blunt scissors to cut the cord at least half an
inch from the navel. Cutting with sharp scissors may require the cord
to be tied first on the pup's side of the cut. We always allow the bitch
to eat the afterbirth as this is the natural way.

If the bitch is a maiden, she may be puzzled when the first puppy
arrives. You must help her by breaking the sac, freeing the pup and
giving it to the bitch to lick and clean. If the bitch still does not realize
what is required, rub the puppy with the towel until it starts to
squeak; mum will usually get the message and take over. One of the
great joys of whelping is to see the maternal instinct rising in the bitch
and how gentle the mother is with her brood.

Whelping can take some time because the time that elapses between producing each puppy usually varies: the second pup may

A drink of water or milk and glucose is often welcomed.

Puppies have arrived with no problems. The bitch has plenty of room in the box but the rails stop puppies being trapped between the bitch and the sides.

Healthy puppies cuddle up together.

appear minutes or a couple of hours after the first. The rule is to keep an eye on the bitch and to prevent her from continuously straining without a puppy appearing. There is quite often a pause in whelping, usually in the middle of a large litter. The bitch will be fairly composed and seem to be gathering strength for the final efforts. It is a good idea to offer a drink of milk and glucose during whelping but do not be surprised if the bitch refuses anything until whelping is completed and she is completely settled with her litter. If the litter is fairly large, keep an eye open when the bitch is having a contraction as she may accidentally crush a tiny puppy against the whelping box. Once the whelping is finished, the new mother will settle down with her pups. They will be clean and shiny, suckling happily and murmuring gently. A happy, healthly litter is unmistakable.

If the bitch is taking her time whelping, we feed the pups with a little glucose and water as most bitches will not want to feed the pups until they have finished whelping.

Complications

Things can go wrong during whelping. The cardinal rule is to call veterinary assistance before the bitch becomes too weak. We also get the bitch checked if there is no sign of labour commencing within three days of the sixty-third day. Bitches can go longer than three days and have no problem but it is better to be safe than sorry. If the bitch is late starting to whelp, your vet may give her an injection to induce birth if this is required; or you may be told to let nature take her own course for another day or two but you do need this type of informed decision for the sake of your bitch's well-being.

Caesarean

If your bitch cannot start whelping for some reason – maybe she has gone into labour and has a puppy stuck that she cannot produce without help – the vet may decide on surgical intervention and carry out a Caesarean section. The operation is precisely the same as it is for humans and the surgeon will perform the operation either by entering mid-line or through the flank. The uterus is then opened, the pup or puppies removed and the incision closed. The bitch is normally completely healed in ten days. This is a very straightforward operation and there is no need to get upset. My wife normally takes the bitch into the surgery and attends to the pups as they are freed from the bitch. We take a cardboard box with a warm bottle and a blanket for the pups and a rough towel to dry them with and to get them active. However, it is probably true to say that most vets are reluctant to allow strangers into the surgery and will present you with a drowsy bitch and pups at the end of the operation. The next step really depends on how alert the bitch is. We like her to be fully awake before putting the pups back with her and you need to do this as soon as the bitch will accept them. We have had a few Caesars over the years, not many with our Boxers but a fair number with other breeds and we have never had any trouble getting pups back onto the bitch.

Failure to Produce Milk

In the event that the bitch does not produce any milk, you will have to cope with feeding a litter of hungry puppies yourself.

Your dog cupboard should contain a premature baby's feeding bottle – we always use a bottle rather than a tube. There are a number

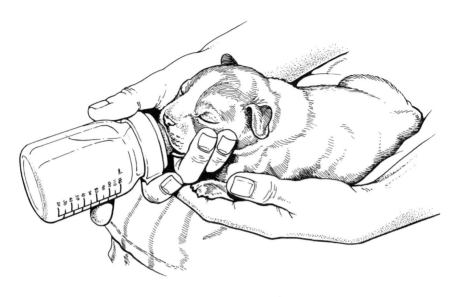

Bottle feeding. The bubbles indicate that the puppy is taking milk.

of powdered milk formulas especially for new puppies, and obtainable from your vet or from a good pet shop. However, it is important that you use a reputable brand. We have had success with mixing a teaspoonful of condensed milk to about a third of a pint of warm milk; if the pups do not seem to be thriving on this, we increase the amount of condensed milk. Bitches' milk is richer than cows' so ordinary milk does need some fortification. Pups need feeding little and often. Their tummies are not very big so you should be prepared to feed every four hours for the first two weeks and from then up until weaning, you can feed the late feed, say, towards midnight and the first feed at around 6.30 a.m. so you can get at least a few hours sleep. As long as the bitch is with the puppies and is cleaning them you should be all right if you keep the feeding going.

Hand-Rearing

If the bitch has not accepted the pups or if you have lost the bitch during whelping so that you are bringing up orphans, you have another duty to carry out: when the bitch licks and cleans the pups, it has a massaging effect which causes the pups to urinate and defecate.

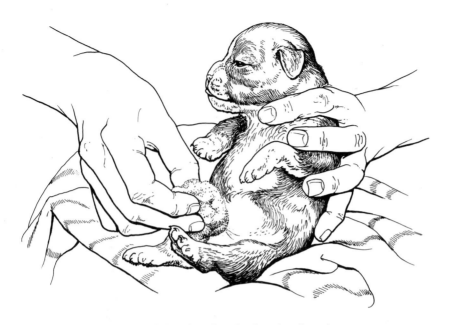

Lint or cotton wool dipped in baby oil used to simulate the effect of the dam's tongue stimulates excretions. This is a most important part of hand-rearing.

In order to simulate this action, you need some soft lint moistened with baby oil. Gently stroke the pups' rectum, genitals and tummy until the pups pass something. You need to do this after every feeding.

It is not difficult to bring pups up on the bottle. Do not forget to feed warm milk, either proprietary milk powder or cows' milk enriched by condensed milk. Watch for the bubbles rising through the milk to show the pup is feeding (we put our fingers each side of the dummy teat and stroke it with a little pressure from the fingers when stroking towards the pup's mouth to give a little help to the slow feeders). Help the pup to carry out its natural functions as explained, be prepared to lose a bit of sleep and you should have no trouble.

Mastitis

During the time the bitch is feeding the pups and especially during weaning, run your hands along her underline and see that none of

Check that eyes are clean and not weeping. Use prescribed ophthalmic ointment where needed.

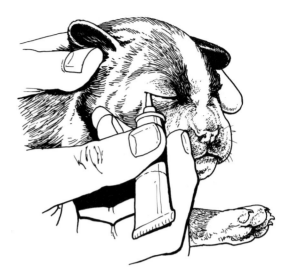

her mammary glands are hard, hot and swollen. You should do this at least once a day and if the teats are getting swollen let the pups take some milk or even do a little hand stripping. If a teat gets really solid you can try hand stripping and bathing with warm water but you should get professional advice or else a nasty abscess can form and your bitch may even have to have a mammary gland removed.

Eclampsia

In nearly forty years of breeding, we have had only one case of eclampsia, but it can occur at any time that the bitch is suckling her litter. The basic cause is an acute lack of calcium caused by the bitch having to supply sufficient calcium to the pups. The symptoms include the bitch behaving abnormally and the first indication is often panting and the bitch looking worried. She often appears to move with a stiff gait and may stumble about. The next stage is collapse as though she is having a fit; convulsions will commence with violent trembling or violent kicking. The spasms pass but are repeated at shorter intervals.

Eclampsia requires emergency treatment to save the bitch's life. Although it is fatal in a very short time the condition responds very rapidly to treatment. Your vet will treat the condition with calcium injections and the improvement is normally spectacular. Most authorities recommend early weaning of the litter to reduce further heavy demands on the bitch.

Vaginal Discharge

Vaginal discharge can be a good indication of incipient trouble. We were always taught that a greeny black discharge during whelping showed the presence of a dead puppy and although this can be true, we have seen such a discharge with a normal whelping. It is normal for the bitch to lose a little blood following the whelping but any reddish brown or foul-smelling discharge could indicate a retained dead puppy, a retained afterbirth or some form of metritis. Urgent attention is needed before general septicaemia sets in with fatal results.

Metritis

Metritis is an inflammation of the uterus caused by infection and can lead to pyometra or pus in the uterus. Open pyometra causes a vaginal discharge; closed pyometra causes no discharge but the bitch's abdomen shows swelling. The only real treatment is a hysterectomy which should be carried out as soon as possible since the bitch's chance of recovery is greatly reduced if the condition becomes toxic.

Retained Placenta

When the puppy is in the womb it is attached by the umbilical cord to the placenta or afterbirth. The puppy is expelled followed by the afterbirth and you should see the bitch pass the same number of afterbirths as puppies. Sometimes the afterbirths follow the pups but we have seen a number arrive together following the birth of the litter. A retained afterbirth spells real trouble and you should get your vet to check if any doubt exists.

Inertia

A bitch can be carrying a large litter but shows very weak or no real contractions when all other indications show that she should be whelping. This condition is called uterine inertia and the name is self-explanatory. You need professional assistance: sometimes a drug injection can start things off but otherwise your bitch will require a Caesarean section.

Still Birth

It is remarkable how the flame of life can appear in an apparently dead puppy. If a normal-looking whelp appears to be born dead you should check to make sure it is actually dead. Try rubbing around the chest and heart with a towel, be quite vigorous with the rubbing and watch for the tell-tale gasp that indicates that life is present. We also gently swing the puppy by the hind legs to try and clear any fluid or obstruction from the breathing passages. A little local heat can often help – try a drop of brandy on the pup's tongue. It is a real source of pleasure to revive an apparently dead pup and see it grow into a sound, happy Boxer.

False Pregnancy

Perhaps one of the most disappointing things to occur is when everything seems to be going well and the bitch seems as though she is going to have a good litter, but nothing happens. This condition is not uncommon in the Boxer breed. We have had bitches who have been absolutely sure that they are to become mothers, even to the extent of scratching up bedding and producing milk. They then contract like a deflating balloon and that's the end of that. One of our bitches would take objects like a sock into her box and nurse it like a puppy for a few days. There is no reason why a bitch prone to false pregnancy should not have a normal litter next time around.

Your bitch should show a healthy appetite when feeding her litter. Should she go off her food, become restless or appear worried in any way, do not hesitate to call your vet as it could be that she is suffering from one of the postnatal problems discussed in this chapter.

Your bitch should soon recover from the whelping. You may find that she loses her coat but good food and exercise will soon get her back into top condition. It is not fair to your Boxer to overbreed her. We always miss at least one season before mating her again and normally take only three litters out of a bitch and only as long as the litters were normally whelped. We would not breed from a bitch who, for instance, showed uterine inertia or problems caused by a constructional abnormality. Any bitch could get into trouble with an abnormally large litter or breech presented pups so a Caesarean operation need not necessarily disqualify such a bitch from your future breeding programme.

With all the warnings and problems I am highlighting you may go off the idea of having a litter. However, probably over ninety percent of litters are absolutely trouble free but you must be aware that trouble can arise and be ready to rectify these troubles before they become catastrophies. Experienced breeders develop a type of second sight for trouble developing. The important thing is to look at your bitch, watch the pups and get help if you see anything that looks wrong.

9

Bringing up the Puppies

When you first examine the new litter, make sure there are no obvious disabilities. We used to have problems with cleft palates and harelips some years ago but this problem seems to have disappeared with the very short heads. Eyes will be sealed shut at birth, noses will be pink; you can see which ones are red and which are brindle; white markings can be seen but these tend to shrink with age. If any of the puppies appear to be sickly or suffering from abnormality, seek veterinary advice.

If you wish to have the puppies tails docked, it will have to be done at three days old. There are moves to make docking illegal and you may have difficulty finding a vet who will perform the operation, in which case, contact a Boxer breeder and ask for help. I shall not give instructions on how to dock puppies as I feel strongly that this is a technique that needs teaching and practical demonstration to carry out properly. Puppies are not to be experimented on. When the

Eight-day-old puppy. As yet, no black pigment on the nose and the eyes are just starting to open.

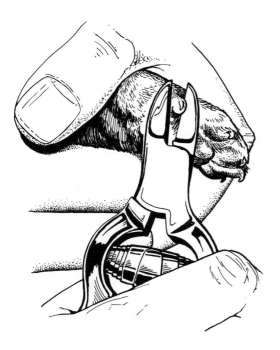

Removing dew-claws three days after birth.

puppies are docked, it is most important that dew-claws are removed at the same time: dew-claws left intact can cause some very unpleasant injuries through getting caught in something and tearing a ribbon of skin away from the leg. It is much safer to have them removed (*see* the diagrams above and below).

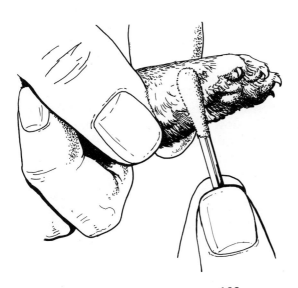

Applying permanganate of potash to stop infection or bleeding.

Undocked puppy. Note the tail carriage.

I am very squeamish when it comes to docking but it is my impression, bolstered by medical evidence, that a puppy feels very little pain at three days old: a little squeak and they are back on their mother and suckling quite happily. There is no doubt that tails are docked for cosmetic reasons; the original reason for docking tails and cropping ears was to allow less grip when fighting. I do have a sneaking admiration for cropped ears having owned three cropped imports but I am delighted we do not crop in this country; cropping cannot be compared to docking as it is carried out at a later age and is certainly not pleasant for the dogs. There are moves to make cropping illegal in some of the countries that still allow it and it is likely that cropping will be banned everywhere in the future. At present, we dock at three days. It would be almost impossible for an undocked dog to win in the show ring and, as a result, they are never seen competing. The situation is only likely to change if docking is banned in this country or the Standard revised to prohibit it.

Especially during the first few days after whelping, the bitch will need peace and quiet and is likely to get quite aggressive if strangers are allowed to look at the puppies while the mother is still nursing.

104

Keep puppies' toenails short to save the dam from being scratched and in preparation for later grooming for show.

This aggression is a very natural response in motherhood and disappears as the litter gets older. Without disturbing the mother, keep an eye on the puppies: they should all cuddle up together and soft, drowsy murmurs tell you all is well. If a pup gets pushed out and the mother is not interested in it, you have got a problem and will probably lose that puppy. We have tried to hand-rear such puppies but have invariably found something to be wrong with them. The last one we had did not have an anus, an uncommon problem although we always check pups for this now.

The pups' eyes will open at around ten days old. When they are fully open, you should check the eye colour which should be a deep blue or violet, indicating a dark eye when mature. A light blue eye gives grounds for concern only in top show prospects. The other thing to check for at this time is a black or dark border to the third eyelids indicating that the dog will have fully pigmented third eyelids – another desirable point for top show stock.

Weaning starts at around two and a half weeks. To begin with, we offer the pups a little scraped or finely minced meat. The pups should take this quite easily from the fingertip; if they do not, try again in a day or two. When they are taking meat, you can start them on milk

First look at the outside world. Wooden platform to lie on and to act as a step.

and cereal (usually at about three weeks of age). By this time the pups should know what a dish of food is for and the main problem is stopping them from getting into the dish with their food. Just keep pulling the pups back from the dish until they get the idea. Once the pups get going, there is rarely any trouble feeding them. You will notice that while the bitch is feeding the pups, she will do all the cleaning required; once you start to help her by feeding, the bitch will stop cleaning the pups and leave it all to you. Do not be afraid of handling the pups. In fact, it is most important that you do since it will allow them to become accustomed to people and also to grooming and being handled in the show ring later on.

The pups should feel full of life and energy and squirm quite strongly. An inert pup should start the warning bells ringing: it may be sick or even suffering from fading puppy syndrome which is a very serious condition. Veterinary advice should be sought immediately.

One reason for starting to wean as early as the pups will happily take food is that the pups develop sharp claws and teeth like needles and can start irritating the bitch's mammaries. The bitch will also start to vomit up her own food if you leave weaning too late.

When the pups are weaned, they should be on four meals a day. A pup has a small stomach so little and often is the rule. The usual pattern is two milky and two meaty meals. The milky meals would be warm milk and cereal, the meaty meals would be minced meat or tripe and puppy meal, the puppy meal is normally mixed with boiling water and left to cool before feeding. It is always difficult to suggest amounts to feed since the demands of individual puppies vary as they grow older. The basic rule is that they should eat all their food at one go. It is difficult to get pups too fat when very young but control the food level when older so that they do not become obese.

As the pups get older, their stomachs develop and you will find that the demand for four meals a day drops off: the food is not attacked with the same enthusiasm. We gradually reduce the meals so that they are eating two a day at around six months. There is no hard and fast formula for feeding but you should regulate food to keep the condition of the dog right. Correct feeding and exercise will ensure that the dog is reasonably well covered and has good muscle tone rather than layers of fat.

Many people feed adult dogs once a day and there is nothing wrong with this; a feeding regime of this type would be normal in the wild. However, we prefer to give a main meal followed by a smaller one later in the day, which we feel suits our dogs best, especially for the kennelled dogs in the winter.

Our adult dogs seem to thrive on about 2lbs of minced tripe mixed with a good quality dog meal and we do not change the diet unless we are forced to by shortages. Dogs do not relish changes in their normal diet and if we do have to change the food pattern we usually get upset tummies and messy runs to clean up. We add some cod-liver oil to the food, multi-vitamins and calcium during growing and teething periods.

If you are feeding and caring for your puppies well, they should develop fairly quickly. The eyes open at ten days, blue in colour, before gradually turning dark brown at about six months. Pups will start losing their needle-like first teeth at three to four months, sometimes later. The permanent teeth which push them out are much blunter and do not cause as much havoc to your ankles as having a mouthful of needles clamped to you when a young puppy decides to give you a playful chew.

Bringing up puppies is an art and while some people get a reputation

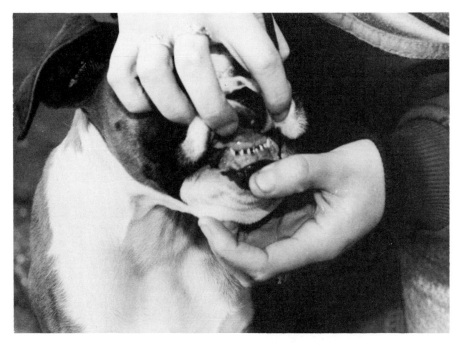

Mouth of a four-month-old puppy who still has the first set of baby teeth, which are just like needles.

for good puppy rearing, others never seem to get pups into peak condition irrespective of how much money or time is spent on them. I think a good rearer gives individual attention to each pup, which means that there is a limit to the number of puppies that can be really well raised.

Do not forget to worm the puppies. We start at three weeks of age and again before the pups go to their new homes. Make sure that the worming treatment you use is suitable for puppies. If in doubt, consult your vet.

10

Choosing a Puppy

An average litter is around six or seven in number, brindles and reds, some plain and some with white markings, males and females. You may also find that you have one or even several white pups. To make their selection, most people start by looking at the pups at birth and assessing colour: the plain puppies are best considered as pets. It may seem hard to discard plain pups just because they lack attractive markings particularly since the Standard does not insist on or even

White Boxers cannot be shown but make good pets.

109

ask for white markings. In fact, the basic Boxer specified in the Standard does not have white markings.

However, in the tough competition of the show ring, you really need your Boxer to catch the judge's eye and even to be chosen in the final selection, a plain Boxer has to be very good indeed and it is most unusual in some countries, including Britain, to make a Champion without some markings. We have tried for many years to breed a plain Boxer good enough to make a top winner but have not been successful so far. The catch is that while white markings can be most attractive, too much white can mean disqualification. The type of markings you want are described in the Standards and can be seen in the photographs of the top dogs. White markings seen at birth always shrink as the dog develops. A narrow blaze between the eyes can disappear altogether but do not expect miracles: a wide blaze that includes part of the eye, a half-white head, or large patches on the body will probably reduce the highest quality puppy to an attractive pet. Brindle or fawn, the choice is yours but always remember that you are looking for the best puppy and colour preference should not affect your judgement.

Fawns come in different shades from light yellow through brown to deer red, the deer red is very popular and can make a very handsome dog. Brindles have the same base colour as the fawns but should have clearly defined stripes. Some dogs are very dark and look almost black but it is always possible to see brindling if you look. The very dark brindles, set off with acceptable white markings, are very popular in some countries and can look very striking indeed.

The Standard does not permit white Boxers. If you have one in your litter, you may have to make one of the more unpleasant decisions involved in breeding. Most breeders do not like talking about culling but I will be honest: if I have a large litter, and more than the bitch can be expected to bring up properly, I have white puppies put to sleep as soon as the bitch has finished whelping. They are taken to our veterinary surgery to be put down properly. Never attempt to do this yourself as, at the very least, it can only compound everyone's distress. Culling is often justified by the fact that white puppies are usually larger and stronger than the other puppies and tend to push the other pups away from the milk bar, which could be considered a weak excuse. Sometimes we have a request for a white pup and if the litter is no larger than six, we will keep the white puppy with a sense of relief that we do not have to do anything about it, but special care is taken to ensure that it is a genuine home and that the puppy will

110

not end up unloved and unwanted. Do not give white puppies away. Set the price lower than you would for a plain pet but not excessively so. This is not being greedy but a test to make sure the prospective owner really wants the pup – if they cannot afford to pay for it, they cannot afford to feed it! You should always be totally honest with the buyer and explain that the puppy cannot be shown. It is certainly preferable to sell white pups unregistered so that they cannot be used for breeding as you do not want them to end up at a puppy farm. There is some suspicion that white Boxers are prone to deafness but I have never experienced this.

You can assess head shape very early – before the eyes open – and you should look for balance of muzzle and skull. Do not worry if the noses are pink as the black pigmentation appears later. When a puppy feeds you can see if it has an ample neck and also how the neck fits into the shoulders. The topline should be level and the tail set on high; quarters should show some angulation but can look a little straight at this time. You really need some experience to assess pups at this early age; an experienced breeder can sort the good from the bad but cannot really say how good the good will be when mature. Some people are remarkably accurate in assessing puppies at birth. My wife is much better than I am and I am not sure if it is a good eye for a puppy or feminine intuition.

At about six weeks old, you can better assess the more likely prospects as you can see them move at this time. First look at the puppies on the floor. You want to see them move with confidence, heads and tails up. Take them away from their usual environment and give them a little while to relax after which the puppies should be inquisitive and explore their new surroundings. Beware of the puppy that hides in the corner: you may have temperament problems with that one. We always have one of the house dogs around so that we can see if the puppies are bold enough to try and make friends with him. You will probably find that one of the pups keeps catching your eye. It may be its confidence, the way it moves or the general look of quality. I usually find that I pick my puppies while they are running around.

The next stage is to stand the puppy on a table. Do not forget to put a mat on the table to prevent slipping. Setting the puppy up is similar to when you are showing in the ring. Gently lift the front and lower it onto its front legs so they are perpendicular to the table; set the back end so it drops into a natural stance and stands balanced. The puppy should have well-barrelled ribs and good bone. The front may look wide at this stage but should be quite straight. The feet should be well

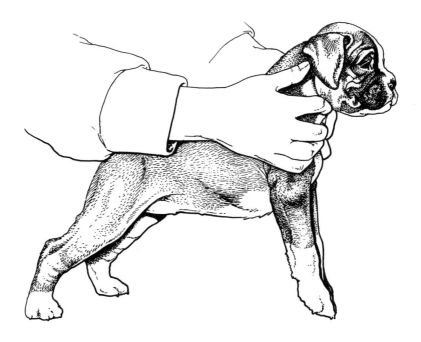

Setting up a puppy for training and assessment. First, set up the puppy's forequarters.

Next, set up the hindquarters.

*Puppy standing in balanced position. Check for level topline, good
tail set and correct front and rear angulation.*

padded and the front feet should have short toes; the rear feet can
have toes that are a little longer. You can check the topline and the set
of the tail; the puppy may roach its back because it resents being
made to stand on the table but you can also check these points by
watching it move on the floor when you can see its natural topline.

Check shoulder placement. You are looking for some layback of
shoulder and length of upper arm. Look for length of neck in proportion to the body. It is worth pointing out that a fat puppy always
looks less elegant than a thin puppy and you need to take this into
account. When assessing the head, you are looking for balance between skull and muzzle. I like to see a dome on top of the skull at this
age; the head should rise between the ears in a triangular shape.
Skulls without this tend to go coarse in our experience. The muzzle
will look a little strange, the top showing a hook, that is, looking
at the topline of the muzzle from the side the end of the

113

*Front is good: straight legs;
arched feet with short toes;
not too narrow nor too wide
in front.*

*Check rear: straight legs;
short hocks; good width of
back and spring of ribs.*

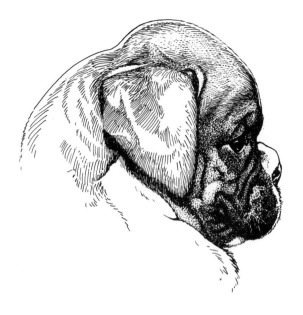

muzzle looks as though it has been pushed down towards the chin. You must see the stop clearly defined and rise of skull even at this age. The eyes should be changing in colour by now and you should be able to check they are the correct shape and that they are placed well. You should also check that third eyelids are pigmented. Ears will look

Head has nice dome on skull and small ears. Third eyelids (inner corners of eye) have black rims so will be fully pigmented. Black pigment is spreading on nose. Muzzle has width and depth; good chin and lip placement. A promising puppy.

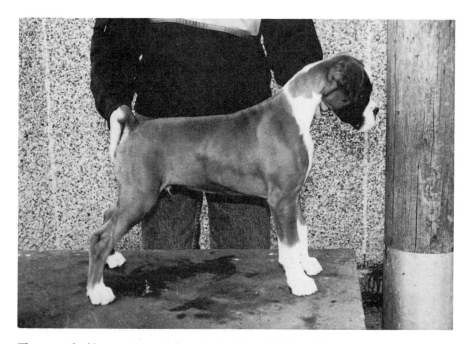

Three-month-old puppy dog with lots of style. Note slight knuckling over of foreleg, which is not uncommon at this age.

large at this age as puppies tend to grow into their ears as they get bigger. The head will look a little long but the skull should show flat cheeks and should never give the impression of being round or apple shaped. Beware of the short head as this can look too short when mature. Gently open the puppy's mouth and you will find that it still has its baby teeth, just like needles! Mouths are difficult but you should look for width. The teeth may look bowed rather than straight at this age but we have found that the permanent teeth can come through straighter than the baby teeth. The bite is usually level or slightly undershot in pups. The lower jaw tends to become more undershot with age. If the puppy has a definite chin, the lower jaw should develop and end up correctly undershot.

Finally, if it is a male puppy, roll him onto his back and check that there are two testicles. If you see only one or none, find out if this particular puppy's line tend to be late developers in this respect. The cryptorchid males always seem to have super heads as puppies but can be heartbreakers if the testicles do not appear later. It is difficult to give advice on this subject although you should probably sell these

*Nice type of puppy dog at a year old. Good forechest and topline;
very strong rear with good width of second thigh and a good neck.*

Clean front: no bulges over shoulders; strong, straight bone in forelegs and good width of front.

Same puppy, as illustrated above. Good rear: clean and taut; broad back.

puppies as pets. However, we did have a dog whose testicles did not descend until he was eight months old and he became a UK Champion. I would say that it is best to keep going with a cryptorchid puppy who is promising in every other way but be prepared to part with him if the testicles do not descend. This all sounds very complicated but, with practice, becomes reasonably easy. We usually learn puppy picking through bitter experience. To begin with, you may wish to seek another opinion, in which case, it is worth asking the stud dog owner's advice. Breeders are busy people so do not expect them to travel to you but offer to make a visit bringing the puppies with you and you will normally find you will get all the help and advice you need. Most of us love seeing puppies sired by our dogs but you may not get the same welcome from a rival breeder. It is difficult to assess puppies from a different line of breeding and you did pay your stud fee to someone else. The owner of a popular and

Seven-month-old puppy dog. Good balance of skull to muzzle; ears look large; chin needs to develop.

119

Same puppy, as illustrated on page 119, at eighteen months old. He still has good balance between skull and muzzle; ears are now the correct size.

successful stud usually has a waiting list for puppies and may well help you to sell your puppies but this is a favour and not an obligation. Never ask another breeder to help sell puppies that have nothing to do with him: the breeder's clients have booked pups from his line and not from anyone else's.

Even after taking advice, you may find that you cannot decide between two puppies. We often find this. Be prepared to continue with them until you can decide which is the better prospect. You can then sell the other one.

Having made your choice, you now need to keep your nerve. You will find that your beautiful puppy will turn into an ugly duckling. Puppies do not grow evenly but in bursts at intervals. Ours tend to look long and low but as long as they have plenty of bone in the front legs, we know they will square up and look balanced at six months. Some pups grow like weeds and then develop body and fill out. Feet

Pretty puppy bitch at three months.

Same bitch, as illustrated above, at eleven months.

121

A very promising four-month-old puppy. Nice topline and rear angulation with low hocks; good bone with growth bumps on front legs. Good shoulder placement and good upper arm and forechest. Note how the neck fits into the shoulders.

and pasterns can look awful and it is best not to worry too much or look too closely at this time. Toplines can look as though they are made of elastic and movement is all over the place. The pup will cut its second teeth around four months of age and will probably get untidy ears and loose-looking eyes while teething. You can check that teeth are coming through properly, straight and wide and you can also check that the pup's jaw is not going to be too undershot and show the lower teeth. The skull always seems to look too broad until the muzzle pads out although if the head looks round, you probably have a real problem. The top of the skull will still look domed and will not flatten until later. The front will gradually tighten and will lose the impression of width that you get with a baby puppy. The topline will firm and movement will start to co-ordinate. If all goes well, your puppy will develop along the right lines and you will suddenly find that your ugly duckling has turned into a swan.

11

Training

Training can be divided into two parts: one part is turning your puppy into an easy dog to live with; the other is teaching it to give its best in the show ring.

The whole basis of training a puppy is to win its confidence and teach it the meaning of 'Yes' and 'No'. We never physically chastise a puppy, even if it tries us almost beyond endurance. The tone of voice used is all-important: a sharp 'No' when the puppy is wrong and lavish praise when it does as you want. A little bribery in the form of titbits is also useful. Once you have established this type of control, the rest is relatively easy. With experience, you will find that you can train your dogs to basic standards without any conscious thought.

When you arrive home with your first puppy, it can be a stressful time for you both. The puppy will have to adapt to a new environment and you will have to cope with the noise and mess. For the first few nights in its first home, the puppy is likely to howl persistently. This is understandable since it will be missing the companionship and warmth of its mother and litter-mates. One way of keeping it quiet is to allow it to sleep on your bed, which can seem a good idea at the time but you are likely to regret it in the future. A fully grown Boxer sharing the marital bed can lead to all sorts of problems, not least of which is lack of space. It is far better to be firm: give the puppy a warm bed (a cardboard box is ideal); one of the older type, stoneware hot water bottles can help if you can find one; and some people find a ticking clock helps (to simulate the heartbeat of its mother). It is surprising how soon puppies will settle down but they are like children: once you give way the battle is lost.

House-Training

Boxer puppies tend not to make a mess in their beds so breeders usually lay down newspaper for pups to mess on. Lay down some newspaper by a door leading to the outside. Once the puppy realizes that it should use this, you can gradually move the paper out until it performs outside. A puppy is most likely to want to go first thing in the morning and following meals when you should take it into the garden and give lots of praise when it does its business. The other thing to watch for is when it starts sniffing the floor and moving in circles: this is the warning to take it into the garden. If you do get a mistake indoors, clean up the mess and give a wipe over with disinfectant, not only for hygiene reasons, but also to destroy the scent so that it is not encouraged to use the same spot again. Be patient. Boxers are naturally clean and do not take long to get the message.

Lead Training

We start lead training at three months old. This is limited to the garden at this age: proper road work starts about two months later. We start off by using a small, medium-link check chain as a collar,

Correct way to put on a check chain. Running link below lead link so that the chain will slacken when the dog is not pulling.

Incorrect way to put on a check chain. The running link is above lead link.

which does not choke the pup but does give some control. We never use leather collars. The dogs do not wear collars at home and are always accompanied when walking or running free. It is a matter of choice whether you use a leather collar or not but if there is any possibility of the dog getting loose, a collar and identity disc is essential. Check chains should not be worn round the home. They can be dangerous if the dog gets loose and can actually strangle a dog if a freak accident occurs. In order to ensure safety and effectiveness, it is important that a check chain is worn and used correctly (*see* the illustrations on pages 124–6). We are lucky and have plenty of fenced space for the dogs to run free but if we had less space we would use collars.

Put a collar on the pup and let it run about and get used to it. There may be some resentment at first, head shaking and scratching, but the puppy will soon settle down. When the puppy has relaxed, clip a lead to the collar, the pup will usually respond by giving a first-class imitation of a bucking bronco. Let it simmer down and end the lesson. When it has accepted the collar and lead, the next lesson is to

Check chain is fitted correctly. Note that this is only correct if the dog is to walk on the handler's left side. If the dog is to walk on the right, the process would have to be reversed.

guide the puppy gently in the direction you want it to go (which is usually opposite to the way the puppy wants to go). One little trick you can try is to pick the puppy up and set it down some little distance from the house. It will usually run towards home and the first battle is won. Be patient and never lose your temper. When it responds correctly, give plenty of praise and the pup will soon get the idea, enjoy itself and look forward to its walk. Do not let the puppy pull on the lead: check it with the lead and control it to make sure that it walks beside you. It is no fun to be towed along by a fully grown Boxer. Lots of praise, and use of the sharp 'No' to check the puppy if it misbehaves, should get the desired results.

It is important to train your dog to use the gutter to foul. No one likes to step in a pile of dog muck and anyone who does is likely to become another convert to the dog-hating league. You should watch your puppy and move it to the road or gutter if it shows signs of squatting. Ideally, you should have a plastic bag and scooper to clean up any mess, especially in public places like beaches or playing fields. So many of these facilities have banned dogs because of a few inconsiderate owners.

Other Training

Another common problem is the dog not returning when you have let him off for a run. Never chase the dog: he will think you are playing with him and you will never catch him – he will be much faster and agile than you are. Our method is to call the dog and walk away from him, which usually brings him back. No matter how annoyed you are, praise him when he returns and give him a titbit. If you scold the dog, he will think you are annoyed because he has returned and you will compound the problem.

An important point to remember is that you should only scold a dog when he is actually misbehaving: it is too late when the damage has been done. The dog will not associate your annoyance with the misdemeanour so will not know why he is being punished. The voice is very important in training a dog. At home, a sharp 'No' if he climbs onto the best furniture will soon cure such problems. We also give the dogs a toy to play with and something to chew. Do not blame the dog if you continually leave him at home and he wrecks the house. Such behaviour is usually caused by boredom and if you cannot look after your dog properly, you should not have one! An older dog can be trusted to look after the house with no problems but he will still want and need your company so you should not leave him alone regularly for long spells.

If you have any problems with training your dog or you want to do more than the basic training, join your local dog training society where you will learn more advanced training and could develop an interest in competition or agility. Letting your Boxer roam the streets is not only dangerous and antisocial but can result in your dog being stolen for dog-fighting use. The Boxer is a strong, brave dog but would be torn to pieces if matched with a highly trained fighting dog such as the American Pit Bull Terrier – the thought of such an end to your loved pet should fully bring home your responsibilities to your dog. Turning a dog into a well-balanced, charming companion is similar to bringing up a child: build up mutual trust, lay down the rules and use patience – the end product is well worth it.

Training for Show

All dogs need the same basic training but show dogs require special education for the show ring. Owners starting in the show ring put

Typical UK Championship Show. Note the dog benches behind the show ring. Your Boxer must learn to relax on these benches during the show.

themselves at a great disadvantage if their dogs are not correctly handled but cannot understand why they are not getting success. If you visit a few shows, you can see how the dogs are shown and learn to emulate the handlers; this requires some experience for yourself and some training for your dogs.

The ideal show dog will show himself: free standing, alert and interested in everything going on about him. A free-standing dog shows this way because of his temperament, which is one of the reasons we look for temperament when picking a puppy. If your pup has retained his showy nature, you should encourage him during road work: stop occasionally and throw something and when the dog responds by standing up and looking, give him lots of praise. Be careful with this, though, as you do not want over-keen or aggressive dogs. Laying too much importance on a showy temperament can produce dogs that are over the top: too keen and a nuisance to their owners and other exhibitors.

Basic show training actually starts when you first set your puppies

You must train your show puppy so that it does not resent being handled by the judge.

Puppies must get used to being shown outdoors or indoors.

on the table for assessment. You should continue to do this regularly so the pup gets used to being handled. Do not forget to open its mouth, look in its ears and pick up the feet so that you will get no trouble in the future when the judge wants to inspect your dog fully. It is a good idea to get other people to go over your puppies to get them used to being handled by strangers at an early age. When the pup is too large for the table, you should transfer it to the floor.

The main fault in handling pups and young dogs is treating them as though they are fragile. Do not be rough but handle them firmly yet gently and never lose patience. Such handling will give the dog confidence. Training to stand correctly is needed however you intend to handle the dog later on; it is the fall back position if the dog is a little off form and will not respond to other methods of handling. Show conditions can dictate the method of handling that you use. Large entries in small rings can make loose-lead handling a real

Topping and tailing a ten-month-old puppy.

Controlled stand.

problem to the other people in the ring. Certainly in the UK, we tend to use more control when handling the dogs.

The most controlled method of handling is 'topping and tailing'. It is probably the most difficult type of handling to carry out properly because the dog must still look animated and it needs a really well-constructed dog to look right. Start by setting up your dog so it is perfectly balanced. Loosen the check chain so that it is slack – you do not want to strangle the dog – and hold the chain by the slip ring; gently put the lower loop of the chain under the dog's jaw. Throw something in front of the dog to make him alert and then gently lift the tail with the other hand. Persevere until the dog responds when set up. If he has the correct temperament and is well balanced, you will find that he will lean into the chain, arch his neck and look good. Some dogs will not respond to this type of handling: they lean back and look terrible. If you are not satisfied with the end result, use a

131

Free standing. Baiting with titbit. Tail needs to be up for perfection.

different method of handling. While practising, a mirror fixed at the correct height and distance so that you can see how the dog looks is very useful when training a dog to show.

When handling, do not dangle the dog by his head and tail. When you lift and position the chain, make sure that you do not bunch up loose skin under the jaw. Hold the chain at a point about six inches above the dog's head while allowing the head to assume a natural position. It is incorrect to pull the head up and back giving a vertical neck position and an ugly angle where the neck joins the topline. There is no need to pull the dog's head off; a well-balanced, and responsive dog would show itself off on a piece of thread. Stroking the tail upwards will teach a dog to lift his tail without your having to hold it. Do not forget to slacken the lead when the judge looks at the head otherwise you can make the head look cheeky and over-wrinkled. Some judges do not like dogs being shown by this method so it is advisable to train the dog to show in another style as a fallback.

The easiest method of handling a dog under controlled conditions is to take advantage of a Boxer's zest for food. Set the dog up so that he is balanced (always the starting point when handling apart from free showing); you then bait the dog. Baiting the dog means getting him on to his toes by showing him something to catch his interest. Well-cooked liver is a good bait since the smell will also attract him. Start by getting down behind the dog and showing him the bait. Firmly insist on the dog standing and using his neck without leaping forward and taking the bait. When you have practised this, you can change to standing in front of him and baiting from that position. When the dog stands and looks at the bait, it almost gives the effect of free standing. One point to remember is that you should bait the dog and not stuff it full of food; when the judge looks at the head he does not want to see a handful of liver hiding the dog's head, saliva flying in all directions. Always check your dog to make sure he is not blowing bubbles or has strings of saliva hanging from his mouth.

Second handling (when someone standing outside the ring attracts

Handling with a loose lead. Again, tail up would improve.

American, Japanese, Canadian, Bermudian and International Molloser Champion, Jacquets Urko, surely the most titled Boxer ever. He is also a great sire.

the dog's attention to help it to show) is forbidden in the UK. Some countries are more tolerant of second handling than others. We see little attempted second handling in Boxers but it can give an unfair advantage. However, it is perfectly fair and acceptable to have someone standing on the other side of the ring so that you can look across to get an indication of whether your dog is standing correctly. It is not always easy to be sure yourself when you are standing over the dog trying to keep him on his toes and you can get your dog standing like a rocking-horse without realizing it.

The whole key to show training is to set the dog up as a young puppy and keep it going. It is also very important to get the dog used to being approached by strangers of both sexes and having his head and body handled; this should also start at as early an age as possible. Use your voice to control the dog, give lots of praise when the dog responds as you want it to and never lose your temper.

As you progress with your show training programme you also need to train the dog to move correctly. You have already carried out

Dogs must be trained to move smoothly. The handler should step out.

lead training so this should not present a very great problem. Judges will ask you to move your dog so that his movement can be assessed and it is to your benefit if the dog moves smoothly at the optimum speed. A car usually has an optimum cruising speed when it runs with the minimum noise and fuss and dogs are similar: though it varies with each dog, there is a speed at which he can achieve the greatest possible co-ordination and smoothest gait. Get someone to move your dog so that you can watch for the optimum trotting speed: the trot is the gait the dog should assume when moving in the show ring. Dogs can usually be moved a little faster when showing side gait than when showing straight movement away from and back to the side. The dog should move on your left-hand side, as profile movement is usually judged in an anticlockwise direction; and you can also change from straight movement into profile movement with no awkward changing the dog from one side to the other. It can be quite upsetting when your perfectly trained pup gets very excited at its first show and starts jumping about when moving but, again, be patient. Judges are usually prepared to give young pups time to settle down and get rid of some of their exuberance. Do not train away all the natural animation. Be gentle and firm and you will end up with a dog who moves with the gaiety that can catch the judge's eye.

12

Showing

The preparation for showing your dog starts right back at the beginning when you are planning your litter or acquiring your puppy. Having carefully reared the pup, carried out show training and propery exercised your show prospect, the time fast approaches when you enter your puppy's first show. If you join your local breed club, you will find that informal matches are held at regular intervals, usually once a month; you can go along with your pup and enter at the venue. You will probably find that the evening starts with a session of show training and then goes on to a knockout competition. These matches are good training and fun for you and your dog.

More formal shows require entering before the date of the show. Shows are advertised in the canine press; you need to study them and decide which you want to enter. You then write or phone for a show schedule which gives details of the show: what classes there are for your breed; details of the variety classes you can enter and compete with other breeds; the date and venue of the show; and the judges of the various classes plus other general information. The schedule will also contain an entry form which must be filled in and sent back to the show secretary with your entrance fee. This must reach the secretary before a specified date otherwise your entry will be returned.

The schedule needs careful reading. The various classes are given and the conditions for entering classes. Classes may be limited to age groups, such as: puppy (six to twelve months); junior (up to eighteen months); veteran (over seven years). You can find classes limited by the dog's winning record. For example, maiden (no first prizes except in puppy classes), debutante (no first prizes at Championship Shows); these classes may also be affected by the various grades of show where the prizes were won. As you see, it can all be rather complex so you need to read the rules very carefully. Generally, you should only enter your puppy in puppy classes otherwise you will be giving away too much in age and maturity to competitors in more senior classes. When you have decided on the classes you want to

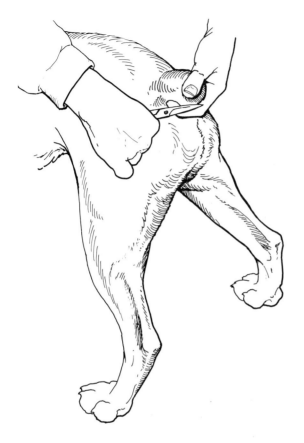

Tidy your dog's tail and do not forget to trim the backs of the legs.

enter, carefully fill in the entry form, making sure all details are correct. You can be disqualified from any wins if you do make a mistake in details on the entry form.

A good feeding programme should result in a Boxer in excellent condition and coat; proper exercise will have given good muscle tone and your dog will move as well as his construction will allow. In other words, you have brought your pup up to its fullest potential and it is meeting the promise you or its breeder had noted and anticipated. The vegetable or cod liver oil you have added to the diet has given a rich gloss to the coat that cannot be achieved with fancy shampoos or tonics.

The Boxer is a smooth-coated dog so you should trim his whiskers with scissors or electric trimmers. Use round-nosed scissors so that the dog cannot damage himself if he moves suddenly during your trimming session. Remove all long hairs, including those that grow

137

The Boxer is a smooth-coated dog. Long bristles on the muzzle need to be removed.

down the back of the hind legs (the ridges where the different lays of the coat come together) and trim the top of the tail. The aim is to show a smooth-coated dog and not an impression of a grizzly bear. By all means bath the dog before the show using an oily shampoo but ensure that you rinse thoroughly to remove all traces of soap. The old trick was to rub olive oil or coconut oil into the coat from about two weeks before a key show and then to bath the dog in an oily shampoo the day before the show. We might do this in a very hot dry summer if the coat is very dry but good feeding and a spot of good hairdressing when you arrive at the show should be all that is required.

At the Show

When you get to the show, check that the dog is correctly trimmed, in particular the bristles on the muzzle which seem to grow very quickly. Give a quick wipe over the white markings with a chalk block, but make sure that you brush the chalk out because it is supposed only to clean the white area and not to colour it. If your dog has unpigmented third eyelids that tend to redden with excitement you should use standard eye drops for dogs to remove the redness; eye drops are also handy if the show venue is very dusty and the dog's eyes become irritated and bleary.

You will have allowed yourself ample time to get to the show so that the dog can be correctly tidied up and prepared and then allowed to relax and take exercise before his class is due. Try and encourage your dog to relieve himself before you go into the ring. Some of my most embarrassing moments have been spent standing in the ring while everything has stopped because my dog needed to relieve himself at an inconvenient moment.

It is important to dress sensibly for the show. It is the dog you are showing not yourself. High-heeled shoes are not really suitable for showing a really super mover who can cover the ground.

When you get into the ring, try and look as though you are at home; you may lose a point or two if you look too much of a novice. Look up the number of your dog, and tell the ring steward what your number is; if you have not already done this, he will have to look it up for you and tell you. You will need either a ring number clip or a safety pin to fasten your ring number where it can clearly be seen. Most people tend to pin it on the left hand side of the chest. It is important to display your ring number so that the spectators can look up your number in the show catalogue and check the details of your dog. Watch the judge's pattern; see where the dogs are stood for individual assessment and the way the dogs are moved. Watching the judge can give clues to what is being looked for in the dogs and help you to decide whether to work on the head and expression or ensure that the dog is standing absolutely right at all times.

We also carry one of the plastic lemons filled with diluted lemon juice which is used when the dog is panting from excitement or because it is hot. A little squirt into the dog's mouth will help to keep his mouth shut while the judge checks expression.

Handling is covered in Chapter 11, (*see* pages 127–35). The main point is that showing is a battle of wits between you and the judge: the handler tries to show the animal's good points and hide his faults while the judge will be noting the good points and looking for any faults. If you are in a small class, the judge will probably place you in order straight away but it is usual to do some refining in a larger

Handlers come in all ages and sizes. This one is really concentrating.

class. Keep your eye on the judge and be ready to come out if the judge wants you. When you have been finally placed, take your win or loss with good manners; remember that dog showing is only a sport or pastime – not a matter of life or death!

Shows always have on sale the show catalogue which is compiled from the entry forms and gives details of all dogs entered at the show. The details include the exhibit's sire and dam, the breeder and the dog's registered name. Always mark up your catalogue so that as you build up a library of catalogues, you can use them as a valuable breeding reference when looking for a stud dog or a breeder who is producing the type of Boxer you like. You should also study the judging, and see what points the judges are looking for. This can help when deciding whether you want to enter under a particular judge again, or which of your dogs that judge is likely to prefer.

When you get back home, get the dogs settled and feed them if they need it. Go through the catalogue again and look for that judge's pattern. Remember any exhibit you really liked and check its breeding. Over a series of shows, you may see a pattern building up that indicates that you should consider using a particular dog for one of your bitches. Finally, update your dog's show records; you need good information on the dog's winning record to be sure of which classes your dog can enter in the future. In the UK, there is an award called the Junior Warrant which is given to a dog who amasses twenty-five points from show wins. In order to claim such an award, you will need a record of the dog's wins and the show and classes where the wins were obtained.

If you are a UK exhibitor and you have had a good win you will look forward to reading the critique on your dog in the canine press.

13

Assessing the Boxer

All Boxer breeders are continually judging their dogs. This may be informally, when evaluating their own stock or puppies, or formally in the show ring. In either instance, the basis for judging must be the Standard tempered by experience.

First, look at the dog as a whole. Is he a typical Boxer or is he untypical? Is he so lacking in breed characteristics that you can mentally dismiss him? You can measure proportions by eye much easier if you can stand back from the dog; it is very difficult if you are standing almost on top of him. From this distance you can assess overall balance, see if he has the correct length of foreleg, and whether he has a good neck or a short one showing an ugly break where it fits into the shoulders. Look to see if the dog has forechest: if the forechest is lacking and the neck does not flow into the shoulders, suspect a shoulder fault. Also, check that the brisket is the correct depth, that the under-line shows correct tuck-up, that the hindquarters are nicely angulated and that the tail set is correct. Look for the very difficult combination of substance and elegance: if the dog is too elegant he is probably too terrier-like in type; if it has too much substance, he is too bully in type. As the correct balance in substance and elegance is very difficult to achieve perfectly, you may have to decide which you personally prefer, a shade light or a shade heavy. These are the sort of decisions that any judge is faced with. We have never seen the perfect dog as yet and I am convinced I never will. At this stage, you are assessing balance and nobility and the more obvious breed characteristics.

Having finished this first inspection, I walk to the front of the dog, still not approaching him and look at the expression to see if he looks at me like a Boxer should – straight in the eye. Next, look at the front to see if the forelegs are parallel with each other and that the front feet do not turn in or out. If the feet turn in he will probably show some looseness in shoulder as he moves towards you; if the feet turn out the dog may be tied in the shoulder and turn his legs apart as he moves towards you. From here, you can also check to see how clean the shoulders are: if the dog is carrying excess weight on the shoulders, make a mental note to check shoulder angulation.

You can then look at the dog from the rear, looking for correct straightness of hind legs. See that the hocks do not turn out (barrel hocks) or in (cow hocks). Look to see that the dog has a broad back and good width of pelvis and from this angle, you should also look again to see that the shoulders are clean and not heavily loaded in comparison with the ribs. Notice that you have got quite a long way through your assessment without touching the dog. You should have a mental check-list of the possible faults and the general quality and balance of the dog. With experience, this takes a relatively short time. You can now approach the dog – always from the front. I always introduce myself by letting the dog smell my hand and giving his head a rub or pat. If you are nervous of dogs, forget about judging – the dog will sense it and may resent you. I have judged hundreds of dogs of different breeds and have never been bitten; I believe that it is a question of being confident that you will not be bitten – so you are not. One dog did grasp my hand in his mouth in the heat of the moment and I still remember how ashamed of himself he was when he realized it was a hand and not another dog but he did not even leave a scratch.

Having approached the dog, check the expression and balance of the head, that the muzzle is not too light for the skull, that it has depth and width and that the lips meet correctly (showing teeth or tongue is a very serious fault). You can look at the finish to the mouth and muzzle and have a good idea of what to expect when you check the bite. Look into the mouth and check the width of the lower jaw: make sure it is not wry, nor parallel with the upper teeth; check that the lower jaw is correctly undershot and that the teeth are strong and correctly separated. There should be six incisors in both jaws, we seem to have little problem with missing teeth apart from incisors but if you want to check all teeth, the easiest formula is:

Incisors $\frac{3+3}{3+3}$ + Canines $\frac{1+1}{1+1}$ + Premolars $\frac{4+4}{4+4}$ + Molars $\frac{2+2}{3+3}$ $\frac{\text{Upper Jaw}}{\text{Lower Jaw}}$

The total number of teeth is forty-two: twenty in the upper jaw and twenty-two in the lower jaw.

As Boxers are active dogs and enjoy pulling games, you may find some incisors missing. You can usually tell if the teeth have been lost or if they never existed: gaps are left by lost teeth. Older dogs sometimes have teeth ground down to the gums and I do not heavily penalize this if the gum formation indicates that the bite was acceptable. You can now check the eye shape and colour. Dark brown eyes give the correct expression. Unpigmented eyes are a fault but some countries penalize it more than others. I find them acceptable in a tight eye; the smeary eye with thick haws (third eyelids) does upset expression, although I would accept a degree of unpigmented third eyelids on a dog who, apart from this flaw, was better than another.

In countries that do not crop ears, you would look for neat ears that are correctly placed and not too low on the skull; if you are judging cropped dogs you would look for a balanced trim with the ears standing correctly. The USA usually has a longer crop than most other countries. Check to see that the head is not heavily wrinkled. A dry head with folds at the root of the muzzle is what is wanted although the dog can show light wrinkle on the brow when on the alert. The head should have a dark mask, which should not extend up over the eyes or the dog will have a gloomy expression. Do not forget to check the nose which should be big and black with open nostrils, properly pigmented without pink markings (known as a butterfly nose). Now look at the head in profile. Check stop and rise of skull and see that the tip of the nose is higher than the root of the muzzle. My final check of the head is to attract the dog by making a noise and checking that it has a bright alert expression. I do love to see a Boxer respond to a stimulus, it is a good indication of temperament.

You can now transfer your attention to the front. If you suspected a problem from your initial inspection, for instance, a loose front, see that the elbows do not protrude. You can gently push the dog off balance and see if anything unpleasant occurs around the shoulder area. Then check the length of the upper arm and feel to make sure that the points of the shoulder blades are reasonably close together. Check the feet and pasterns at this stage: soft feet usually go with soft pasterns; you can check this again when the dog is moving.

Pass your hand over the topline to ensure there are no unwanted bumps. Check the spring of the ribs, check that the musculation is firm and that the dog is in peak condition – the substance should be made up of muscle not fat! Now check the hindquarters. Make sure they are correctly muscled; you are looking for big, strong hams and wide second thighs. See that the feet are tight and well padded but remember that the toes will be a little longer than on the front feet. Do not forget to check that a male has both testicles fully developed and descended into the scrotum (you may give a puppy the benefit of the doubt). You may find a problem here if you find a male who, apart from missing a testicle is excellent in every respect. The UK Standard gives no real guidance on this, apart from a note at the end which says that a male should [and not must] have two testicles descended into the scrotum, and 'should' is weaker than 'must'. Personally, I would find it difficult to place a poor specimen over an otherwise excellent cryptorchid but would find it most difficult to give one a top honour; other people in the UK would take a different line and most other countries would not accept such a dog at a show.

While you are handling the dog, assess temperament. He should not show signs of fear or aggression – this is most important if we wish to retain proper temperament.

You should now have assessed the faults and virtues of the dog. At this stage, I enjoy trying to forecast how well the dog will move. It is usually fairly easy to spot the poor movers; the surprise is when a dog built to move does not go as well as he should. Handling is a battle of wits between the judge and the handler but when the dog is on the move, the best handler in the world cannot disguise the faults.

Your first analysis is with the dog moving directly away and then coming back to you. You should look for straight legs; pasterns should be an extension of the legs and should not toe-in (pin) or turn out (paddle). The elbows should be kept close to the body and should not show evidence of looseness (out at elbow). If an exhibitor does not seem capable of approaching you in a straight line when moving towards you, suspect faulty front movement and insist on a straight approach. Assess the rear movement in a similar way: the hocks should not turn in throwing the feet out (cow hocks), nor should they turn out, throwing the feet in (barrel hocks). The legs will move nearer each other as the dog moves faster, this is not a movement fault but a normal reaction. What you have to watch for is single tracking where the legs **always** move closely together; this is a con-structional point and should be assessed as a fault.

The real test is watching the dog move in profile because the handler cannot fool you and, in effect, the dog is on his own. Watch for smooth, powerful movement. The paws should follow a long flat curve without rising high off the ground at the beginning or end of the curve. Front paws rising high in front of the dog like a hackney pony indicates an upright shoulder or another shoulder problem (you can always recheck to see what the specific problem is). The rear end should generate a lot of drive. Watch for a long, smooth push from the rear legs, even the hocks should show extension. Time spent

145

A Champion on the move. Note extension of front and rear legs. See how the paws stay close to the ground, conserving energy. Topline is held while the neck is used for balance. The whole action is smooth.

waving the paws in the air means wasted power. Watch for the hind legs overstepping the forelegs, which can cause the hind legs to take a different track to the forelegs (sidewinding). This can also be seen when moving the dog directly away from you and usually indicates better rear angulation than front angulation. Dogs with this fault often show an exaggerated slope of back.

Another problem you may notice is the dog sinking between his shoulders when in action. Notice the topline: the dog should hold his topline and it should not oscillate as if made of elastic. If he has a good temperament, the dog should move gaily and show animation, tail held high. I hate to see an apologetic Boxer moving with his tail clamped down. Other things to look for are the dog retaining balance and not pulling himself forward by his forelegs. Again, this can be seen when posed: all the weight is on the forehand and gives the impression that if you lifted his rear he would somersault onto his nose!

You may find that an otherwise well-behaved male will challenge the other males when they get too close, either when posing in line or when moving. You should not penalize a dog for this because it is only natural for a stud dog to attempt to dominate the other dogs. Give him room and try again. If the dog becomes uncontrollable and loses his head, it is not true to the real Boxer character and he should be excused from the ring.

All this sounds time consuming. In fact, it is quicker to carry out than it is to write or read. With practice, you can assess a dog in a few minutes. How to judge a class of Boxers is explained in the next chapter.

14

Show Judging

When you have gained experience in the breed and have bred and shown some good stock, you will probably start thinking about judging some breed classes and making your way up the judging tree. Showing your dog has given you some insight into the way judges go about the job and follow the correct procedures normal to the county you live in. The best way to get a preview of how it feels to be officiating in the show ring is to volunteer to be a ring steward.

Stewarding

Your task as a steward is to keep the show ring running smoothly so that the judge can concentrate on the prime role of judging. As a novice, you will normally be helping a more senior steward, handing out prize cards and other quite mundane tasks, but this is important experience since you will be getting acquainted with the difference between officiating and showing your dog. A senior ring steward has quite a lot of responsibilities: organizing the ring as the judge has requested, making sure that new dogs are in the correct place and are placed in order where the judge has asked them to be. A good steward will also ensure that the ring is tidy and dogs have room to move. Remember that stewards should be inconspicuous, do their jobs and keep out of the way when judging actually progresses.

When judging is being carried out, watch the method used by the judge and see if you can work out the type of dog the judge is looking for. Most judges will talk to you about the dogs if you approach them in the right way and at the correct time. The right way is to be polite – remember, the judge is doing you a favour – and the right time is when there is a period of relaxation between classes. These little discussions and bits of advice are extremely valuable, so do not forget to reciprocate later on in your career when you are the judge.

In our country, there is no formal training for an aspiring judge. It is possible to take a correspondence course and learn quite a lot in this way but you will still need hands-on experience. Many countries run official training courses, a period of study as an apprentice judge followed by written and practical tests. We have an unusual show system consisting of different level shows, the highest level being the Championship shows. This system can allow a judge to make steady progress to the top which is to become a Championship Show judge, approved by the UK Kennel Club to award Challenge Certificates.

Your first judging appointment will probably be at a breed club match. These are normally judged on a knock-out basis and are excellent preparation for more formal appointments. I always found knock-out judging difficult: some unknown law ordains that the best dogs usually meet in the first round and after the first difficult decision the whole thing becomes an anticlimax. Matches are an excellent way to start your judging career and give you an indication of whether you have the temperament to judge at higher levels.

From here, you can go on to officiate at higher levels, through Limited and Open shows until you have gathered the experience, knowledge and confidence to qualify for awarding Challenge Certificates at Championship Shows. In the UK, the Breed Council has specified levels of judging competence based on experience in breeding and judging. When an aspiring judge meets the various requirements, his name is entered on a list of judges who have reached the specified level. This gives a well-defined path to the top. Only the UK Kennel Club can approve judges to award Challenge Certificates; shows that are not at Championship level can invite to judge anyone who the Committee decides has enough experience. Other countries have different methods of developing judges, including theoretical and practical study courses followed by an examination. If you want to know how your national system operates, contact your local Breed Club.

A good judge is made up of many parts and the most basic quality is absolute honesty: lack of experience can be rectified; lack of honesty can never be put right. But honesty by itself is not enough, courage is also required in order to withstand all the pressures that are applied. Pressure takes many forms, from the seemingly innocent remark that a particular dog is very nice but what a pity he has such terrible hind action, to the truly spine-chilling glare that can virtually paralyse you from the other side of the ring. You must be tough enough to ignore pressure of any kind.

Just being honest will solve most of the difficulties you will meet.

For instance, in the event that you are expected to judge a dog by your stud dog or even bred by you, give him a prize if he is good enough. It is equally dishonest to put down unfairly a dog who has some connection with your kennel as it is to put him up! Similarly, if your best friend shows a poor dog under you, place him where he should be – at the bottom of the line. Some countries are relatively small and top-winning dogs are easily recognized. The cardinal rule is that no dog brings his show record, prefix or reputation into the ring. He is just another exhibit and should be treated that way.

It may sound difficult to judge dogs as if you have never seen them before and have no knowledge of their faults or virtues, but it is very easy once you get into the ring: the dogs can look quite different to how they looked from the ringside and you will often find that some of your preconceptions will evaporate. Any judge can tell you of occasions when the major winners have been as much a surprise to them as to the ringside. This question of personal characteristics is very important and it can all be condensed into a very few words: if you want to be a judge be sure that you judge the dogs, not just place them – there is a whole world of difference between the two.

Honesty, integrity and knowledge are fundamental requirements in a judge but there are other points that need to be recognized. People will enter under you because they want your opinion on their dogs; some will come to the show because they want to see the dogs. But you are the ringmaster at the show and you have to orchestrate the proceedings. A good judge will develop a ring technique that will ensure that the exhibitors are happy, the onlookers can follow the judging and everything proceeds in an orderly fashion. Every judge develops their own approach to judging but I will describe a basic approach that you can modify to suit yourself. My theory is that judging dogs is based on comparison: you compare the dogs to the Standard and decide the close decisions by comparing your final selections with each other.

When you enter the show ring, prior to commencing to judge, have a look round and see which is the best way to set up your ring. The spectators will also want to see the dogs so if you have a blank side of the ring, where no seating is available, arrange for your line-up to be that side of the ring. If you judge out of doors, the ring may be uneven so look for a flat piece of ground for the dogs to be set up for individual examination. Take account of the sun's position: it is diffi-cult to assess expression and eye colour when the sun is shining directly into the dog's eyes. When you have decided how you want the ring organized, where the new dogs will line up, where you want the repeat entries to stand and what side you want to judge from, tell your ring steward and establish control over your ring from the first start.

When you are ready, ask your steward to call the class into the ring. It is a good idea to have a quick look at the dogs so that you can get a feel for the general standard. It is surprising how you can see the quality dogs even at this stage. Call your first dog to the position where you have decided you want to carry out your individual examination. This will usually be near the end of the ring so that you will have room to move them. Stand well back from the dog and assess the dog as described in Chapter 13. My pet hate as an exhibitor is a judge who is fumbling with my dog before I have even set him up correctly.

Take your time, let the exhibitor get the dog settled and be very gentle with puppies. When you have finished your examination, ask the exhibitor to move the dog. If the ring has some width you can ask for the dog to be moved in a triangle so that you can see movement coming, going and from the side. A long, narrow ring may require a straight up and back twice and you will have to move to the side to see the dog gaiting. Some handlers will top and tail their dogs (*see* Chapter 11, pages 131–2), so you may want to see him free standing after moving the dog or you may want to check his expression. Do not forget to be courteous and thank the handler before the dog goes to the end of the line. A little advice: try and note some distinguishing feature about the first dog you look at or his handler so that you will know at a glance when you have seen all the dogs. It does not really matter if you call the dog out again but as a judge, you must foster the impression of omnipotence.

If the class is relatively small, say about ten, you can miss the next stage but if you are judging at a Championship Show you may have thirty or more in the ring so I would suggest you carry out a first selection. The individual assessment will have given you an impression of the dogs that interest you, so, have another quick look round the dogs and start pulling out your finalists. The number of dogs you pull out for your final selection will depend upon the quality, but one of the main aims is to clear ring space for the next stage. Having made your selection tell your steward you have finished with the others and they will leave the ring. Tell the remaining dogs to go back into line. You may have to make a further selection as your aim is to end up with a number of dogs similar to the number of places you have to award. This is not an absolute rule: in a high-quality class you may end up with more.

Having got your class down to manageable proportions, you can start comparing the dogs. Again, it is wise to stand back and look at the dogs as a whole, then go in close and look at detail. As the ring has been cleared, you can ask the dogs to go round so that you can compare the gaiting. Line them up again and place them in order. Take any notes you need for your critique (*see* pages 152–5) and you are ready for the next class.

You may find that you get repeat entries in following classes: dogs you have seen in previous classes appear again. It is normal to line these up separately on the other side of the ring in the order that they were previously placed. You do not need to carry out the individual assessment on repeat dogs but do not forget to include them in your selection process. It is possible that a dog shows much better in a repeat class and as all classes should be judged separately, there is no reason why you should not alter your previous placement. Some may criticize you for revoking; others will appreciate your honesty.

When you have finished judging the classes, the class winners return for the Best of Breed contest. If the classes are split, it is normal to judge the unbeaten males first. Select the best male and, possibly, the Reserve best male, depending upon the type of show. The process is repeated with the females and finally you select the best out of the

The climax to a show. Best dog and bitch battle for Best in Show title. Notice that both dogs and handlers are giving their best.

151

top male and top female for Best of Breed (at a breed show this would be Best in Show). The judge can call for a dog only beaten by the Best of Sex for consideration for the Reserve Best of Sex but this is not mandatory. There may also be other specials to award, such as, Best Puppy. At UK Championship Shows, the Challenge Certificates would be awarded to the Best of Sex and Reserve Challenge Certificates to the Reserve Best of Sex. If you judge in other countries, you may find a different system. Judging in the rest of Europe usually requires that all the dogs should be graded and a critique is written on each dog; in the USA, Champions do not normally compete for the points awarded that count towards the Championship title. Some countries also have a minimum age for awards counting towards the Championship title. It would be difficult to cover all the variations so if you have an overseas appointment you need to study the individual system for that particular country.

Whichever way you judge, it is necessary that you follow a pattern. The exhibitors can follow what you want and the show flows much more smoothly than if you change your patterns every other class. A good judge will also keep control of the ring but do not think that you should bark comments like an army drill instructor. Quiet and firm is the right approach. Keep an eye on what is happening in the ring, ensure that handlers keep their dogs under control and do not interfere with other exhibits. Do not allow handlers to pelt other dogs with pieces of liver or squeaky toys. Ensure that the stewards do not dominate your ring. Treat the show ring as if it is a different world and never allow any prejudice to sway your opinions. Be polite and considerate to the exhibitors, they are honouring you by showing their dogs under you and, without them, you would not have anything to judge. Dress smartly and sensibly: the dogs are the stars, not the judge.

The task of judging may include writing a critique on the major prize winners for publication in the dog press. This is essential when judging in the UK and you should not accept an appointment if you are not prepared to give your impression of the dogs afterwards. Other countries have different approaches: some require critiques and grading for each dog; some countries have no requirement at all for critiques. You need to check the requirements for any country that asks you to judge and follow the methods for that specific country.

The requirement to write an individual critique is a good discipline because it does teach you to really look at a dog point by point and some practice at this is very good for any judge. Many other countries

Keep your dog looking good while the judge is writing his critique.

put much more emphasis on assessing movement as the dog goes round the ring but the very large entry common in this country does make it difficult for the judge to spend much time gaiting and writing critiques for each animal.

In the UK, it is normal to give an assessment of your top winner (or winners, depending on the level of the show). Championship Shows require that the first and second in each class is critiqued, Open Shows would require only first-prize winners to be described. As these guide-lines can be changed, do not forget to make enquiries at the time of judging. It is acceptable to start your critique of dogs judged at major shows with a statement of the standard of the dogs, any general faults in the entry and changes that are noticeable since you last judged. Next, you need to comment on your winners and why you have rewarded them. My opinion is that judging is all about recognizing and rewarding the virtues of the breed – any fool can see

153

Very elegant puppy bitch with a lovely outline.

This nine-month-old puppy dog has an attractive head: good eye; good lip placement and chin; big nose; good stop and rise of skull.

faults but it takes knowledge to recognize virtues. Your critique will probably indicate the virtues that you recognized, perhaps qualified by any faults that troubled you. The perfect Boxer is an impossible dream and it is all too easy to pick holes in a good dog and give yourself the unenviable reputation of being a fault judge.

A little humility is also a useful asset. While you are judging the dogs, the ringsiders are judging you and honest judging shines like a diamond in the ring. If you do find that your pattern of winners is far different to the normal, have an agonizing reappraisal and consider the possibility that your idea of true Boxer type may not be entirely correct.

All this sounds more complicated than it actually is. All you have to do is to go into the ring and place the dogs in your order of preference; if you have enough experience and the basic characteristics of honesty and courage, the job is extremely simple.

155

15

Imports and Exports

We have been extremely lucky to have owned two imported stud dogs that proved to be of significant value to the breed in the UK. The question we were most often asked was why we imported the dogs in the first place. The answer is quite simply that we saw virtues in the American dogs, which, at that time we needed in our breeding and which we could not find in a dog in the UK. This is no insult to the British dogs of that time: specific qualities tend to vary with supply or fashion and we felt that our dogs lacked a little in expression, mainly because some British dogs that we otherwise liked had rather oblique eyes with a hard expression or small eyes. One particular line that I had used with success suddenly started using a dog with eyes that were rather light and large; more like door knobs than Boxer eyes.

I had been travelling to the USA on business quite frequently and kept noticing that a dog called Scher Khouns Shadrack was producing Boxers of high quality and of the type I liked. Shadrack's pedigree indicated that he came from a line of top producers and not only was he siring top show dogs but he was also siring top producers. In fact, Shadrack's sire was the great Int. Ch. Milans Fashion Hint with lines back through the top-producing Salgray dogs. Our only difficulty now was to find one of his good sons, if this was out of a top-class bitch, we would have an extra bonus.

A mutual friend put us in touch with Mrs Margaret Krey of Kreyons Boxers, and it was our real stroke of luck that we met and made friends with this most generous and knowledgeable enthusiast. On our next trip to the States things started to move. We went to see Margaret who had two of Shadrack's sons out of her lovely top-winning bitch, Ch. Kreyons Firebrand. Margaret agreed to let us have one of the Firebrand sons called Kreyons Back in Town and we could not wait for Mack, as we called him, to arrive in the UK. Of course, we had to quarantine him for six months: he did not enjoy it and, in spite of everyone's efforts, came out looking more like a greyhound than our hopes for the future.

American import, Braemerwood Proclamation of Seefeld, a sire of Champions in three countries.

Ch. Witherford Hot Chestnut exported from the UK to Germany where he set up a great record as a top show dog and sire.

Margaret had been generous over the sale price of Mack. In fact, she really made it possible for us to own the dog. However, the cost of flying the dog to the UK plus quarantine was quite a heavy investment so we were anxious to see what he would sire for us. We knew he was a proven sire having fathered a litter in the USA before leaving the UK. Our first litter duly arrived with three good-looking bitch puppies. We kept one and the others went to well-known kennels. When the pups came out at the British Boxer Club Championships Show and went first, second and third in a huge puppy class, breeders realized that quite an important dog had arrived. Mack went on to sire four British Champions and many overseas Champions. The litter he left behind in the USA contained Rainey Lane's Grand Slam who went to Australia and sired nineteen Australian Champions. Mack's great strength was that his offspring had lovely expression. He did what we had wanted and passed his lovely eyes on. He usually managed to help upgrade puppies from all types of bitches and the lovely expression that was his trademark could be recognized in his descendants.

158

Later, we made another trip to the States and met Major Valarius Kluger who asked us to have a look at a red male he owned. It was the day before we were due back in the UK so we were a little reluctant owing to the lack of time. However, we met at a motel car park in pouring rain and saw this magnificent red male, showing his head off despite the foul weather. The dog was called Milray's Red Baron of Valvay and he was closely inbred to Shadrack, again from a direct line of top producers. My wife had judged Boxers during this trip and had really liked some bitches that were Baron's litter mates.

We loved the dog and thought he would make an ideal mate for Mack's daughters. We were delighted when he asked us if we really wanted the dog and when I replied 'Yes, but . . .' he put the lead in my hand and said, 'He's your dog'. What wonderful people Boxer people are. Where Mack's qualities were more obvious to the expert and expressed through his puppies, Baron was all flash and style

Kreyons Back in Town of Winuwuk. An influential sire with many Champion descendants worldwide. A lovely portrait by the late Marion Fairbrother.

159

Winuwuk Milray's Red Baron of Valvay. American export to Britain. British Boxer Club's Sire of Merit 1982 and runner up, 1981.

together with many virtues. He became another successful stud for us who sired British Champions. We mated one of Mack's daughters to Baron, and a puppy in the litter, an elegant brindle, looked so good she picked up the name Good Golly. Golly had the lovely breed type Mack handed on plus Baron's flash, style and showmanship. She still holds the record for top-winning brindle bitch in the UK. Mack, Baron and Golly have all gone now but our present Champion male is a son of one of Baron's top-winning daughters, so the line goes on. One of our great prides is to look through the pedigrees of many top-winning dogs at home or overseas and see Mack and Baron in their background.

We were very lucky to import two top stud dogs. First, we picked dogs of excellent breeding from top-producing and winning lines. Then we saw the dogs ourselves and could see exactly what we were getting. Luck also came into it in that we met two very kind people who made it possible for us to own the dogs. I suppose we followed the advice given in the chapter on genetics and reaped the benefits.

160

Ch. Kreyons Firebrand. Best in Show and Futurity winner. Dam of Back in Town.

The other side of the coin is when your Kennel becomes well known and people from overseas contact you asking for a good puppy, usually a dog for stud purposes. You now have a real responsibility: you must remember that you are being asked for a dog who can be used to upgrade or retain the quality of the breed in another part of the world. Any dog you send overseas should be at least as good as a dog you would retain yourself for similar purposes. The price you ask should be exactly the same as you would charge in your own country. The new owner will have to pay transport and may have to put the dog through quarantine – a very high price to pay for a second-class dog.

Before arranging to export any dog, you should check with your local officials, depending upon your country of origin. In the UK, you should contact the Ministry of Agriculture and ask for the rules and regulations for sending a dog to the country in question. You will probably require certain inoculations and veterinary certificates. Travelling boxes or crates have to be a certain minimum size depending on the size of the dog and these details can be checked with the airline agent. Your customer should have checked the quarantine requirements in the country of destination and accommodation should be booked where required. All these details should be checked before the dog is shipped. Once the dog has left the country there is no way back, except through quarantine where necessary. The great thrill that makes all this trouble worth while comes when you get a phone call telling you how delighted the new owner is with the puppy. You can also enjoy its show career and if all goes well, a breeder's certificate if the dog gets his title. It has given us great pleasure to visit some of the countries where our dogs have gone and

Canadian Champion, Lounsbury's Flashback, now at stud in England.

to feel proud that the dog looks good. It must be humiliating to see a very poor dog who has cost a small fortune in purchase price and transport costs.

We have been delighted when visiting other countries and found that the Boxer imports have generally been of good quality and an asset to the breed.

16

Advertising

Although dog breeding is primarily a hobby, it is not often that all the pups in a litter are good enough to keep. Selling your surplus puppies is a useful way of subsidizing the costs of feeding and showing your stock. Another source of income arises when you are lucky enough to own a top-class male: if the dog is good enough and has good breeding, other breeders will want to use him and the stud fees can help your expenses.

You can wait for the world to beat a path to your door but if you do, you will be left with a lot of puppies or a very seldom used male. You will be trying to make a sale against competition so you need to be prepared to market your product, in this case, puppies or studs.

If you have followed the advice given in finding a puppy and selecting a sire, you will have a litter of well-bred pups, which is your first advantage over some of your competition. The owner of a stud dog will always be interested in a litter sired by his dog if it is out of a good bitch and can often help you sell the puppies by putting you in touch with prospective customers or purchasing the pups for resale. There is no obligation for the dog's owner to take your pups, it will depend on demand, the quality of the pups and the way the pups have been reared. It is good manners to let the sire's owner have a look at the pups before most of them are booked; you will not find much interest if all the good pups have been booked and the poorer specimens are left.

The first litter is usually easy to sell: friends and neighbours who have admired your Boxer often want to own one just like yours. If your litter does not go as fast as you expected, you have some decisions to make. It could be that you are not asking the right price: over optimism in setting the price can easily result in lost sales. Lots of prospective buyers with no actual purchases is a pretty good indication that your prices are too high. Check around locally to see what the market line is. You really want to see the pups gone at around eight weeks, insisting on high prices can easily see the erosion of your meagre profit by extra feeding costs. The usual trap here is to insist upon the same price as you gave for the dam. There is a cost premium involved in purchasing a puppy from a kennel with a high reputation compared with a breeder who is just starting out so be realistic, sell your pups at a fair price and do not exaggerate the quality to justify a higher cost. You will surely see that puppy in the show ring and you want to be proud, not embarrassed, as you build up your kennels' reputation.

If you find that there is not a lot of direct interest in your litter, you will have to make sales by advertising. The investment you make in your advertisement should depend upon the quality of your litter. A nice litter of pet puppies can usually be found good homes at reasonable prices by using the classified columns of your local newspaper. This will reach the people who are not sufficiently involved with dogs to purchase one of the specialized dog papers. Local sales do have the advantage that you can have a good look at the prospective buyer and ensure that the puppy is going to a good home. Again, put a fair and reasonable price on the puppy and do not radically drop the price. We never haggle over a pup's selling or buying price because one of the ways to help ensure that the pup will have a good home is to make sure that the buyer can afford to keep it properly. We have also found that when we have responded to a hard luck story and let a pup go cheaply, that puppy is an instant candidate for Boxer rescue.

The contents of the advert should be aimed towards the type of customer you are looking for. Good pet homes are best found by stressing the lovable quality of the pups and the ideal character of the breed. Most of us are a little snobbish at heart so you can stress the pedigree, good breeding and that the litter is Kennel Club registered. Selling very high-quality pups requires a different approach to your publicity: you need to stress the excellent breeding of dam and sire (this may be more important for the dam because the sire is probably well known to other breeders). In effect, you are now doing the reverse to finding a good pup, so stress those points that you looked for in a pup. Do not fill your advert with superlatives; this is a real switch off to most buyers.

A similar approach is used to sell the services of a stud dog. A record of wins and a show title will focus attention on the dog and will bring in some casual enquiries. The acid test of a stud dog is not what he has won in the show ring but what he puts into the whelping box so you need to highlight the dog's stud record as a producer of sound, quality stock. If he is bred from a top-producing line then tell everyone. Chapter 6 on selecting a stud dog will give a good indication of the strengths that a breeder looks for. Again, avoid superlatives. People part with their hard-earned money for facts and not hot air.

Good wins also deserve a little publicity: your new puppy starting its show career with a good win; your dog gaining his Champion title; your show dog siring a top winner – show events such as these are always worth a little investment and go towards making your Kennel's reputation. A bit of good publicity can always help to ensure that a judge will appreciate that your animal is a winner; a lot of publicity can ensure that a lot of judges will recognize that your dogs are winners.

One of the most useful publicity aids is a good photograph. So many times you see a good dog badly photographed. People actually pay good money to publish these unflattering photographs of their dogs and wonder why the advert was a total flop. The other point is that most people will jump to the conclusion that if you cannot judge a photograph of your own dog, you cannot judge other peoples' dogs; not entirely true of course but a bad photograph is many times worse than no photograph at all; and a good photograph can tell a story that a hundred words cannot. The basic rule is to highlight the dog's virtues: if he has a lovely head use a head shot; if your dog has a super outline, concentrate on that. A really good photographer who knows the breed can flatter your dog by choosing camera angles, lighting or printing to show the dog in his best light. It is well worth using a top professional dog photographer to take that special photograph. The investment will pay dividends.

You can take your own photos. Modern compact cameras are very capable of producing fully acceptable results but there are just a few basic rules to consider. Heads generally look best if you take a photograph from an angle that shows one and a half eyes, that is, one full eye and the other at the edge of the skull. Outlines look best if you take your photograph from near the ground. Setting up your dog facing the sun can make the musculation stand out so the dog looks coarse; flat lighting with the sun almost behind you will produce better results for the novice. Two other basic rules for photography: get close enough to fill the viewfinder and make sure the background is clear – you do not want a telegraph pole growing up from your dog's head. Above all, if a photo is not good enough, do not use it.

If you have been successful in attracting people's attention, you will get a phone enquiry. The next step is to get your prospective buyer to see what you have to offer. I know the effect of endless phone calls but you need to be as positive, bright and cheery with the seventieth call as you were with the first: the last caller may well be your real customer. We do tell people the price ranges of our available puppies or stud fees of our dogs. These are not negotiable and it can save a lot of time if this is made clear at the first contact. Boxer puppies are so utterly delightful with their comic little faces that they sell themselves but I must repeat one point: look and see if the home will be suitable and try and discover the motive for owning a Boxer. If this is the buyer's first puppy, show him a mature Boxer so that there can be no doubt as to what this comical puppy will end up as. Especially watch the reaction of any children: do they draw back in fear if the puppy approaches them or are they spiteful? If you have any doubts, do not let the puppy go.

If you are offering a stud dog and the owner of the bitch is a novice, have a look at the bitch. See that both dogs do not have similar faults, that she is good enough to breed from and that the pedigree is acceptable with no hereditary fault carriers. This is all part of publicity: a poor litter by your dog caused by mating him to an unsatisfactory bitch can ruin your dog's stud career before it starts. If you like the bitch, get the dog out and show him to your visitors; you can also let them see the dog's good temperament (if he has a bad temperament, he shouldn't be at stud!). Potential users of your dog are always impressed by seeing a few good pups sired by the dog.

Once you have made your kennel's reputation, you will rarely have to advertise. Most breeders of quality stock have a waiting list and it is unusual to have to seek publicity. If you have a large kennel, you may have to invest in advertising to clear the pups but this must add to the cost of the pups making them more difficult to sell so you can find yourself in a vicious circle if you are not careful. Most really good pups are never advertised; they are snapped up very quickly. Stud dogs do need advertising because they are operating in a competitive market and breeders do need reminding that they are still around.

Advertising is a valuable means of finding good homes for surplus puppies and it helps to get your reputation established. If you do advertise, do it properly or the results will be far worse than if you did not look for publicity at all.

17

First Aid and Diseases

The Boxer is normally a healthy uncomplicated dog but, similar to humans, can get involved in accidents or pick up an infectious disease.

There is one problem specific to Boxers that the new owner must be aware of. It is a neurological disease called Progressive Axonopathy (PA). The condition has been shown to be an hereditary disease and the mode of inheritance being a simple recessive gene. The disease takes the form of the degeneration of the nervous system. It affects the hindquarters and manifests itself at a relatively early age. Cases of the disease were confined to Great Britain but three cases have recently been reported in Norway. The mode of inheritance has allowed the problem to be virtually isolated to known carriers and the total cases reported are less than one hundred out of many thousand puppies so a sense of proportion must be kept. The best safeguard is to tell the breeder you want a puppy free of known PA lines. The British Boxer Breed Council will furnish full details in PA by request although I must stress the point that the incidence of this problem is so low and the problem lines so well defined that it is highly unlikely that your Boxer puppy will develop PA, so please do not let this warning put you off a delightful breed.

Inoculations

There are some most unpleasant and serious contagious diseases that all dogs are subject to. These include some major infectious diseases that, in the past, have claimed many dogs' lives. Fortunately, safe vaccines have been developed for protection against infectious canine hepatitis, leptospirosis, canine parvovirus and canine distemper including hard pad. All responsible dog owners should contact their veterinary surgeons and ask for their suggested vaccination regimes which would depend to some extent on the local disease conditions.

Puppies are passed antibodies from their dams but the maternally derived antibodies do decline at a certain age. The problem is that the maternal antibodies, when still present, will prevent correct response to vaccination so you really do need expert advice to ensure that your pup is correctly safeguarded and the immunity gap between the time of decline of the maternal antibodies and the response to the vaccination is as short as possible. Obviously, it is wise to keep your pup away from other dogs or places where they may pick up infection until they are protected. It is heartbreaking to see a puppy die for no good reason. A good vaccination regime with boosters at the correct intervals can almost eliminate the chances of losing your Boxer to these killing diseases but there is always a residual risk where immunization is not fully effective for one reason or another.

Parasites

Internal and external parasites are other cases where good animal care can help the dog and those in contact with it.

Internal Parasites

We are lucky in Britain the internal parasites common to our dogs are mainly roundworms and tapeworms. Other countries have other parasites including hook, lung and whip worms. Your veterinary surgeon will give advice and suggest suitable vermifuges. A very small risk to humans must be pointed out when discussing this subject and that is associated with the common roundworm. The small eggs, if accidentally swallowed by humans, can develop into larvae in the human gut. They will not develop into the adult stage but migrate through the human body, usually causing no problems. However, it is possible that they may settle in the retina of the eye and cause an impairment of vision. The possibility of vision impairment is minute but must be recognized and the correct precautions taken.

Your puppy should have been correctly wormed either by you or the breeder. Worming should have been carried out twice before the puppy is eight weeks old. You should follow a correct worming programme and properly dispose of all faeces. Children should wash their hands after playing with pups and never allow a puppy to lick their faces or mouths. Dogs' feeding utensils should also be kept separate from humans'. I would also add that in spite of the recent

A syringe is useful for giving medicine, worming, etc.

and rather overdue publicity on this problem, we have not experienced nor ever known of any of our dog-owner friends having experienced this problem and my time goes back over thirty-five years.

Roundworms tend to appear in the pregnant bitch. The release of hormones activate the dormant larvae and some of these migrate to the puppies. The larvae arrive in the pups' intestine and rapidly grow into adult worms. Egg production begins when the pup is about two months old so this is the reason for two wormings before the pup is eight weeks old. The usual signs of worm infestation is a pot-belly on a pup that is not thriving, usually with a harsh coat. However, you should not get to this stage if you have properly wormed the bitch before whelping. Always assume that your pups and their dam have worms and take the proper action as advised by your veterinarian.

Tapeworms are usually noticed when the dog passes the shed tail segments of the worm in his faeces. These segments also carry the eggs and look like grains of rice when dried. In extreme cases, the dog will be continually hungry and lose condition. Your veterinarian will prescribe the correct treatment. The eggs that are passed in the dog's excreta or remain sticking to the coat are eaten by flea larvae and will develop into adults if the dog should eat an infected flea. Re-infection will occur unless the dog is kept free from fleas.

External Parasites

External parasites include fleas, lice, ticks, harvest mites and mange mites. A dog who scratches very frequently should always be checked for these parasites. Fleas and lice are controlled by regular dusting. It should be remembered that fleas lay their eggs off the dog in such places as the dog's bed, around the edges of carpets and in upholstered chairs, so it is important to dust the dog and the furnishings; extra effort with the vacuum cleaner also helps. Many dogs can put up with fleas but some can develop an intolerance that can develop into dermatitis. Other signs of flea infestation are the flea droppings which are about the size of a grain of sand, hard and black in colour. Fleas move rapidly and can jump surprising distances.

Lice are slow moving and lay eggs that stick to the dog's hair. As lice actually breed on the dog, you do not have to worry about dusting upholstery and furnishings as you do with a flea infestation. A good insecticidal shampoo will control these pests.

Harvest mites are small, red, parasitic larvae which appear in summer and autumn and dogs pick them up when being exercised on grass. The larvae burrow into the skin of the dog, usually between the claws, and cause intense irritation. The dog will lick or bite the affected paw. Your vet is the best person to treat this problem.

Ticks are my pet hate. The sheep tick is most common in Britain and dogs pick them up when exercised in fields where sheep have been pastured. Ticks attach themselves to a dog by embedding their heads in the dog's skin, where they engorge themselves and swell up to the size of a pea. At this stage, they resemble grey warts. The usual advice is to get rid of them by soaking them with ether or surgical spirits until the tick loosens its hold when it can be removed but great care must be taken to ensure that the head is removed intact. If the tick is forcibly removed, the head may part from the body and remain in the dog's skin causing an abscess. We have always had problems removing ticks and get our vet to remove the really stubborn ones. We are lucky in Britain in that we have no problems with ticks carrying diseases that can be passed on to dogs or humans. In some countries ticks can carry diseases transmittable to humans and in these countries gloves or tweezers must be used when removing them.

Mange used to be a very common problem and old dog books are

171

full of cures of unknown effectiveness. We can split the generic term mange into various types. Sarcoptic (Scabies) is caused by a mite that burrows into the skin and lays eggs which hatch out and repeat the process. The symptoms are persistent scratching and bare patches that typically appear at the elbows, stifles and around the ears and eyes; these patches can spread over the body. The condition is highly contagious so dogs suffering from mange should be isolated from other dogs. The mite can live on humans so it is advisable to thoroughly wash after contact with a dog. The condition responds to treatment and is quickly cured. As the mite can live for a short time away from its host, bedding should be destroyed and insecticide should be used in the places where an infected dog has been.

The type of mange that is most dreaded because of the difficulty of effecting a cure is demodectic mange. The parasite involved lives in the hair follicles so treatment is not easy. The symptoms are loss of hair, thickening of the skin followed by pustules caused by infection of the hair follicles. This stage was known as the 'red mange'. The condition is usually accompanied by a very unpleasant smell and the dog will often appear depressed. Skin scrapings will confirm the diagnosis. Treatment can be given and careful nursing is required but the condition can recur. We have had success with the single case we have experienced but if the dog does not respond to treatment, euthanasia may be necessary to save the dog from further suffering.

Another type of mange is caused by a mite that lives in a dog's ears causing ear scratching and head shaking. The condition rapidly responds to ear cleaning followed by a course of ear drops.

A few of our dogs have suffered with *Cheyletiella* mites. These are small parasites just visible to the naked eye. One sign of infestation is scurf in the dog's coat. If I pick up a dog with *Cheyletiella* I suffer from a rash. This is common to many people; the mites do not seem to worry the dogs but they certainly worry me. Treatment is simple but the full course of treatment must be completed because of the long life-cycle of the mite.

A skin problem that you need to watch for is not caused by a parasite but by a fungus. The condition is known as ringworm and there are a small number of different types of fungi that cause the problem. The symptoms are circular patches on the body where the hair has been lost; the patches can show crusting, especially in the younger dog. The fungus is spread by contact between affected dogs and other animals and humans. Diagnosis is confirmed by checking skin scrapings under ultraviolet light. We had a minor outbreak caused by an infected cat and we first noticed when my wife's neck showed lesions from cuddling the cat. Your vet can supply fungicides that control ringworm very quickly and efficiently. The real nightmare occurs in burning all bedding and treating with fungicide all the kennel areas or places that the affected dogs frequent. The fungi is very hardy and re-infection can occur if stringent precautions are not taken.

The conditions discussed so far are ones that I tend to consider as being controllable with good animal husbandry: they would be noticed and controlled during day-to-day kennel activities. Dogs are active, inquisitive animals and can get involved in accidents or eat things that they should not.

Accidents and First Aid

Every dog lover should have some idea of emergency first aid so that he can help his dog if an emergency does occur. At this point, it must be stressed that first aid is purely an emergency treatment to ease a dog's pain or to help him until professional treatment is available.

When a dog is in severe pain, care has to be taken that you do not get bitten while trying to help him and so you may have to use some kind of restraint. The most common type of restraint is a muzzle. Emergency muzzling can be done with a length of material formed into a clove hitch, which is passed over the muzzle of the dog and tightened. The ends can be brought back over the dog's head and tied to the collar to keep the muzzle in place, or tied in a half hitch under the dog's muzzle and then tied around the dog's neck. We have found that one leg of a pair of tights or a stocking makes a very good emergency muzzle. You can practise with your own dog so you will be conversant with the technique if needed.

Road Traffic Accidents

If a dog has been struck by a vehicle, your first action is to restrain the dog to prevent him from hurting himself further. You can throw your coat over his head and if possible, fit an emergency muzzle. Then move the dog to the roadside as gently as possible. Check the dog's condition, treat injuries as suggested in this chapter, cover lightly to keep warm and get the animal to the vet as soon as possible.

To make an emergency muzzle, take a stocking or leg of a pair of tights and make two loops.

Place one loop behind the other, to form a clove hitch.

174

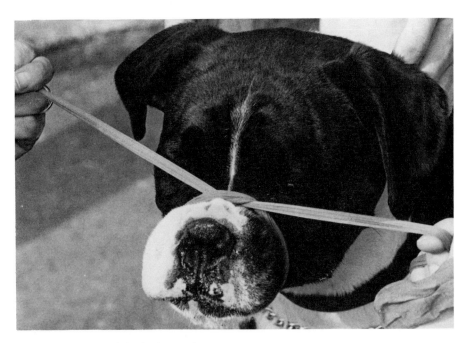

Tighten loops around the dog's muzzle.

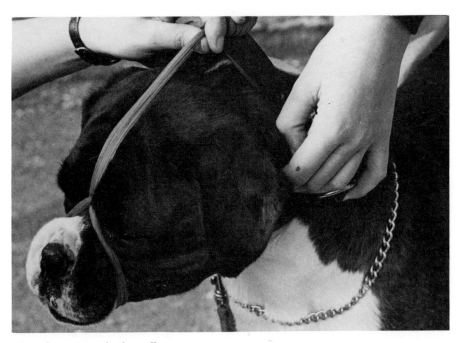

Tie ends to a stout leather collar.

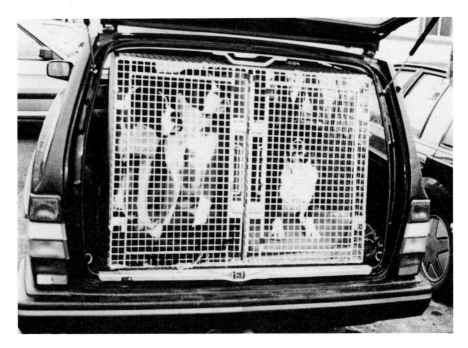

A fitted dog guard keeps the dogs safe in transit and can be lifted out for use at shows.

Fractures

Usually in a limb, fractures and dislocations can be recognized by the way the dog holds the limb or its unnatural appearance. A temporary splint or support can help. A dog should be taken to the vet with the least possible changes in position. If you do suspect a fracture, a flat board used as a stretcher is preferable. Otherwise, carry a dog on a blanket with the four corners brought together to make a sling. Disturb as little as possible.

Bleeding

External   The dog will clean up minor wounds by licking. If the dog cannot reach the wound, bathe it with a diluted antiseptic. Heavy bleeding or dark-coloured blood indicates a severed vein; such bleeding can be controlled by using a pressure pad applied to the wound. Bright red blood that spurts from the wound indicates a severed artery and while a pressure pad can usually control this type of

176

bleeding while waiting for professional attention, you may have to use a tourniquet if bleeding is very heavy (indicating that a major artery has been cut). However, you must remember to slacken the tourniquet every fifteen minutes and keep checking that the limb does not become cold to the touch below the tourniquet. A pressure pad can be made of any suitable, clean material, preferably medical lint, formed into a pad and strapped over the wound. Emergency tourniquets can be made by forming a loop out of material or cord wrapped round the leg and winding it up by using a pencil or similar until the loop is tight enough to stop the flow of blood. The pressure pad method is preferable to a tourniquet as it is less likely to cause other complications.

Internal This often follows a car accident and one visible sign of it is shock. Gentle handling is required and veterinary assistance as soon as possible.

Shock

Shock is an extremely serious and dangerous condition which is brought on by severe stress or trauma, such as experienced by a dog involved in a road accident. The symptoms of shock are collapse, shallow breathing, glassy eyes, rapid heartbeat and weak pulse, cold legs and ears, and pale gums. Ensure that the airway is clear. Lie the dog on his side with head lower than his rear to encourage bloodflow to the brain. Keep him warm and quiet and get professional assistance immediately.

Heat Stroke

It is a continual source of amazement how people who are truly fond of their dogs will leave them in a sealed car in hot weather, which is the major cause of heat stroke. The symptoms are acute distress, difficult, very rapid breathing and collapse. First aid is to reduce the dog's temperature as rapidly as possible: a bucket of cold water thrown over the dog or placing the dog in a cold shower are examples. When his temperature has returned to normal, he should be kept quiet in a cool place. Drinking water should be made available to him. If recovery is not rapid, obtain veterinary assistance immediately as he may need to be treated for shock. As with many health problems, prevention is better than cure and heat stroke kills!

Burns

Minor burns and scalds can be treated with antiseptic ointment. Check the burn to see that the inflammation is reducing. Larger burns may need a light bandage for extra protection.

Severe burns and scalds should be doused with cold water to reduce the pain but no further home treatment should be carried out. The dog should be taken to the vet immediately.

Poisoning

The necessity for first aid for poisoning should be avoided by ensuring that all poisons are safely out of reach of dogs. However, in the event that your dog is poisoned, the important thing is to be able to give the veterinary surgeon some indication of the type of poison that the dog has ingested. There are a surprising number of poisonous substances in general use, or even growing in the garden. Signs of poisoning include vomiting, fits, foaming at the mouth, staggering and coma. Strychnine poisoning which was used for vermin control, results in rigid extension of the neck and limbs. Unscrupulous people still use strychnine poisoned bait so never let your dog near any dead animal found when going for a walk. If you actually see your dog eating a poisonous substance it may be valuable to administer an emetic to make the dog vomit. Mix up a strong salt solution and make the dog swallow it. You still need veterinary assistance at once. Emetics should not be administered to a dog who has swallowed strychnine or any corrosive substance.

Electrocution

The first and most important point is to switch off the electrical supply otherwise you may join the dog! Electrocution is usually caused by dogs or puppies chewing electrical cables. If you cannot switch off the supply, push the dog away from the cable with an insulator such as a length of dry wood, pole, broom or similar. You may need to pull the dog's tongue forward to help breathing and start artificial respiration at once. Artificial respiration is carried out by placing the dog on its side and depressing and releasing the dog's rib cage at the rear of the rib cage at a rate of sixty depressions a minute. Keep this up while waiting for professional attention.

Fainting

We have experienced fainting with Boston Terrier puppies but not in Boxers, although we have heard of cases. The dog is playing happily at one moment and then just keels over. If this occurs, check that the tongue is not blocking breathing and wait for the dog to recover. An isolated instance is not very important but if the fainting persists have your vet check the dog.

Fits

The dog goes into convulsions and kicks and froths at the mouth. The symptoms can be quite upsetting but the best thing to do is to leave the dog alone as long as he is not in a situation where he is likely to injure himself or get injured. You may need to hold the dog down but be careful to keep away from the dog's mouth or it may accidentally bite during the convulsions. Check the duration of the fit and the dog's behaviour during the fit. Fits may be a symptom of other problems and you need professional advice to find the specific problem and its cure.

Wasp and Bee Stings

Not usually a great problem except if excessive swelling occurs – epecially in the mouth or tongue – which may block the airway. Bee stings should be removed and the area treated with a mild alkaline (bicarbonate of soda, for example). Wasp stings should be treated with a dilute acid such as lemon juice or vinegar. Stings to the mouth and throat should be treated immediately by a vet.

Drowning

Hold the dog up by the hind legs to drain any water out of the lungs. Apply artificial respiration as described under Electrocution (*see* page 178).

Eye Injuries

If a foreign body enters the eye or an eye injury occurs, make sure the dog does not aggravate matters by scratching or rubbing the eye with a paw or on the ground. The first sign of something wrong is usually

179

a running eye that the dog tends to keep shut. Hold a pad that has been soaked in cold water against the affected eye and see your vet.

Dog Fights

Most of our dogs' fights are just establishing pecking order and are more noise than fury. Very occasionally we may have a couple of dogs equal in status who actually get to grips. Obviously, the first priority is to separate them and we find that a hosepipe directed at the dogs' heads and noses is quite successful. If one dog does lock a grip onto another, you can still part them with a jet of water up the nostrils or, if the dogs have collars, you can insert a stick through the collar and twist it to choke the gripping dog off. It is best to have two people so that the dogs can be controlled when they separate and before they resume the battle. I have managed to get mixed up with a couple or more dogs fighting without suffering a single scratch: the dogs always seem very aware of which was the other dog and which was me. The worst thing you can do is to panic. Do not rush screaming at the dogs as you will only stir them up more. If a dog has a hold on the other dog, do not try to pull them apart or you can turn straightforward bite wounds into horrendous rips.

Once you have the dogs apart, clean them up and check for wounds. Most wounds are superficial although ears are vulnerable to rips, tears and punctures. Have a good look to ensure that there are no concealed puncture wounds, though Boxers do not have the long, pointed teeth that you meet in other breeds like the Terriers. If you do have any deep bites or rips, you may be in for a stitching session at the vet's with some antibiotic treatment to avoid any infections. Deep puncture wounds are often not stitched in order to promote better healing without forming pockets of infection. Puncture wounds may also require anti-tetanus shots irrespective of how the wounds happened.

Bloat

The full name for this condition is Gastric Dilation and Torsion. It is a sudden enlargement of the stomach caused by fermenting food producing gas. The condition is made even worse when the stomach twists, blocking both the entrance from the throat and the exit to the intestines. The first signs of the onset of this condition is usually restlessness and unsuccessful attempts to vomit, followed by severe distension of the stomach which can easily be seen. The dog shows great distress and various degrees of shock. This is a true and serious emergency. Instant treatment is required before changes take place in the body that are irreversible and fatal. The veterinary surgeon will release the built-up gas but the dog may require surgical intervention to correct the torsion. Dogs at the larger end of the medium-size breeds and above seem most vulnerable to bloat and indications seem to point to the symptoms appearing following exercise after eating a large meal. Cases of bloat have been reported in Boxers but the condition does not seem to be a major problem in the breed.

There are many diseases of all types that dogs are prone to and it is always a temptation to give a list of illnesses, a description of the symptoms and how the condition is treated. I would prefer to give my heartfelt opinion that diagnosis and treatment of canine complaints

Red Baron at eleven years old.

Back in Town as a veteran.

are best left to the veterinary surgeon who has been exactingly trained for many years in the profession. What the good breeder or owner does is watch his dogs carefully and observe any changes in behaviour or physical characteristics. For instance, you need to observe such things as swelling of the abdomen, which could be the start of bloat or could indicate a closed pyometra in a bitch, conditions that require rapid surgical intervention. Lumps and bumps on the Boxer do need looking at and careful watching. If they start to enlarge, something needs to be done about them. Mammary cancers can be a problem with Boxer bitches. Our Boxers tend to live to an average age of around twelve years so we take that into account before surgical intervention: we would not stress an older bitch with an operation if the prognosis was not excellent.

When you have been involved in dogs for a while, you develop a sixth sense about the health of the dogs. My wife frequently baffles me by pointing to a solid, black masked, brindle and saying, 'that dog looks pale'. She is usually right! The dog is a little off colour for some reason. Dogs cannot tell the vet what the problem is: diagnosis must be based on clinical signs. But it will help to get the correct treatment if you can describe any differences you have noticed in the dog that could be due to the onset of a health problem.

Euthanasia

One of the things we can do for our old and loved dogs is to help them on their way when life becomes too much of a burden. I have never regretted having put a dog to sleep when in pain with no cure. I have regretted not having had the courage to make the inevitable decision earlier. It is so easy to rationalize and keep a dog alive for his sake when really it is for your sake. One thing you should do to repay the years of love and faithfulness is to be there at the dog's last moments so that he goes on his last journey without fear. We grieve for our old ones, then go back to the kennel and look at a promising puppy or an expectant bitch, and so the cycle goes on.

I hope you have enjoyed this introduction to the Boxer as much as I have enjoyed writing it. It gives me great pleasure to think that I may be able to give something back in return for the pleasure that I have always had from the finest of all the great dog breeds – the Boxer.

Appendix 1

Boxer Clubs of Great Britain

Anglian Boxer Club
Secretary: Mr V. Zammit
Rhinestone Cottage
Foxes Lowe Road
Holbeach
Spalding
Lincs.
Tel: 0406 24661

British Boxer Club
Secretary: Mrs M. Cattanach
Down's Edge
Reading Road
Didcot
Harwell
Oxon.
Tel: 0235 835410

Cotswold Boxer Club
Secretary: Mr T. Hutchings
'Winuwuk'
Downton Road
Stonehouse
Glos. GL10 2AX
Tel: 0453482 2253

Essex & Eastern Counties Boxer
  Club
Secretary: Mrs N. Sasse
Bluebell Lodge
Rayleigh Down Road
Rayleigh
Essex
Tel: 0702 524049

Irish Boxer Club
Secretary: Mr D. Manton
14 Dillons Avenue
White Abbey
Co. Antrim BT37 OFX
Tel: 0232 863692

London & Home Counties Boxer
  Club
Secretary: Mrs R. Hughes
7 Eastwick Drive
Great Bookham
Surrey KT23 3PP
Tel: 0372 58325

Mancunian Boxer Club
Secretary: Mrs D. S. Hall
251 Ainsworth Road
Bury
Lancs. BL8 2LP
Tel: 061 764 5593

Merseyside Boxer Club
Secretary: Mrs A. Unsworth
344 Wigan Road
Atherton
Lancs.
Tel: 0942 873709

Midland Boxer Club
Secretary: Mrs M. Buck
8 Dugard Place
Barford
Warwick
Tel: 0926 624660

Northern Boxer Club
Secretary: Mrs N. Brook
20 Haworth Avenue
Blyth
Worksop
Notts.
Tel: 0909 76291

Scottish Boxer Club
Secretary: Mr W. Miller
High Kirkland
Leswalt
Stranraer
Wigtonshire
Tel: 0776 87211

South Wales Boxer Club
Secretary: Mrs V. Pack Davison
Sunnyside Cottage
Tranch
Pontypool
Gwent
Tel: 04955 55623

South Western Boxer Club
Secretary: Mrs E. Coombes
Rockleigh
Rock Hill
Halberton
Tiverton
Devon
Tel: 0884 821055

Trent Boxer Club
Secretary: Mrs J. Alton
75 Victoria Road
Selston
Notts.
Tel: 0773 810630

Tyne, Wear and Tees Boxer Club
Secretary: Mr D. Edwards
Kvarner
Broomhill
Houghton Le Spring
DH5 9PT
Tel: 091 2613709

Appendix 2

Boxer Rescue

The Secretary of the Boxer Breed Council, Miss Ann Podmore, is able to give names and addresses of all Boxer Rescue contacts (*see* Home Counties Boxer Welfare).

Miss Ann M. Podmore
Farthing Ridge
89a High Street South
Stewkley
Leighton Buzzard
Beds. LU7 OHU
Tel: 0525 240288

Cotswold Boxer Club Rescue
    Service
Mrs J. Drew
45 High Street
Haydon Wick
Swindon
Wilts.
Tel: 0793 726868

Irish Boxer Dog Club
Mr John Williamson
41 Dhu Varren Parade
Belfast BT13 3FJ
Tel: 0232 240818

Mancunian Boxer Club
Mrs Doreen Hall
251 Ainsworth Road
Bury
Lancs.
Tel: 061 764 5593

Merseyside Boxer Club
Mrs Marjorie Burnett
(Co-ordinator)
640 Leyland Lane
Leyland
Lancs.
Tel: 0772 421946

Midland Boxer Club
Mrs Peggie Ingram
Bockendon Kennels
Cromwell Lane
Tile Hill
Coventry
Tel: 0203 466706

Northern Boxer Club
Mrs N. Slater &
Mrs Waring
28/30 Newlaither Hill
Newsome
Huddersfield
W. Yorks. HD4 6RG
Tel: 0484 533081

Scottish Boxer Club
Mrs Rhonda Watson
(Co-ordinator)
29 Greenvale Drive
Brightson
By Falkirk
Tel: 0324 713511

South Wales Boxer Club
Mr T. Donovan
16 Gwaun Coed
Brackla Estate
Bridgend
Mid Glamorgan
Tel: 0656 50724

South Western Boxer Club
Miss June Grover
Church Farm
Isle Brewers
Taunton
Somerset
Tel: 04608 202

Trent Boxer Club
Mr Barry Alton
(Co-ordinator)
75 Victoria Road
Selston
Notts.
Tel: 0773 810630

Tyne, Wear & Tees Boxer Club
Mrs J. Smith
7 Ventnor Road
Linthorpe
Middlesborough
Cleveland
Tel: 0642 827295

Home Counties Boxer Welfare
Miss Ann M. Podmore
Farthing Ridge
89a High Street South
Stewkley
Leighton Buzzard
Beds. LU7 OHU
Tel: 0525 240288

Norfolk Boxer Rescue
Mrs Heather Smith
The Gables
344 Holt Road
Horsforth
Norwich
Tel: 0603 897555

Cotswold Boxer Rescue
Mrs Pat Banks
23 Cashes Green Road
Cainscross
Stroud
Glos.
Tel: 04536 5251

Devon & Cornwall
Mrs Dorothy Muzzelle
Leburnick Kennels
Lawhitton
Launceston
Cornwall
Tel: 0566 2635

North Wales
Mrs Ellen Shields
1 Hillside Cottages
Dolgarrog
Conway
Tel: 049 269 265

Hampshire/Dorset
Mrs Jean Scheja
Appletree Cottage
Lower Common Lane
Three Legged Cross
Wimborne
Dorset
Tel: 0202 822498

Cheshire
Mrs Susanne Jones
Watling House
Forest Hill
Hartford
Northwich
Cheshire
Tel: 0606 889043

Index

Italic numerals denote page numbers of illustrations.

accidents, 173
Ackendene Kennel, 28
Alma v. d. Frankenwarte, 20, 21
Alts Schecken, *14*
American Boxer Club, 32
American Kennel Club, 32, 33
American Pit Bull Terrier, 127
Awldogg Southdown's Rector, 22

Bang Away of Sirrah Crest, Am. Ch., 22
Banks, Mr and Mrs E., 27
Best in Show, *151*
Best, Mrs M., 28
bleeding, 176
bloat, 180
Bosco Immegrun, *15*, 17
Boston Terrier, 53
Boxer, clubs, 184–5
    rescue associations, 186–8
Brabanter, 13
Braemerwood Proclamation of Seefeld, *157*
Braxburn Kennels, 27
Breakstones Kennel, 21
Breed Council, 148, 168
Breed Standard, American, 33–8
    FCI, 39–43
    first, 30–2
    interpretation of, 47–64
    UK, 44–7
Broughton, Mrs P., 29
Bulldog, 13, 15, 32
Bullenbiesser, 13, 15
burns, 178
caesarean section, 95, 99, 100
car dog guard, *176*

Carinya Kennel, 28
Cartwright, Miss S., 23
Cattanach, Dr B., 26
Challenge Certificate, 148, 152
Check v Hunnenstein, Ch., 20
Cheyletiellamite, 172
Coebes von Westfalenwappen, *53*
controlled stand, *see* handling
Count on Barro, Ch., *58*
critique, 141, 151, 152–5, *153*
cropping, 104, 144
cryptorchid, 116, 119, 145

Dampf v Dom, Ch., 20
Danziger, 13
Davis, Miss M., 21
Dawson, Mr E., 21
demodectic mange, 172
Deutscher Boxer Club, 30
dew-claws, 103
distemper, 168
docking, 103, 104
dog fights, 180
Dogge, 13
Dolf the Buhe Farm of Marbelton, *56*
Dorian von Marienhoff, Int. Ch., *17*, *19*, 20
drowning, 179
Dunkels and Gamble, Mesdames, 21
Dyson, Mr and Mrs P., 21

eclampsia, 98
electrocution, 178
emergency muzzle, *174*, *175*
euthanasia, 183
eye injuries, 98, 179

Faerdorn Pheasant Plucker, Ch., *26*, 27
fainting, 179
Fairbrother, Mrs M., 21, 22, 159
false pregnancy, 100
Faust Vom Haus Germania, 22
Favourite Vom Haus Germania, Dutch
    Ch., 22
Federation Cynologique Internationale
    (FCI), 39
Felcign Faro, 22
Felcign Kennel, 22
Finemeres Flip of Berolina, 22
first aid, 173
fits, 179
fleas, 170, 171
Flock St Salvator, 17
Foan, Mr and Mrs M., 28
fractures, 176
free standing, *see* handling

gastric dilation and torsion, 180
Gayus von Schatzkastlein, *54*
Gestation, 88, 89
Gigerl, Ch., *14*, 17, 18
Glenfall Kennel, 29
Great Dane, 13, 53
Greenway, Mr and Mrs P., 28
Gremlin Kennels, 21
Gremlin Summer Storm, Ch., *23*, 24, 26
Grover, Miss J., 28
Grysett von der Goldquelle, *52*

Hambleton, Mr and Mrs J., 26
handling, controlled stand, *131*, 132
    free standing, *131*
    loose lead, 133
    topping and tailing, *130*, 131, 150
    see also second handling
hand-rearing, 96
hard pad, 168
harvest mites, 171
heat stroke, 177
Heath, Mrs P., 22, 67
Helios Vom Haus Germania, 22
hepatitis, 168
Holger von Germania, Ch., 22
Horsa of Leith Hill, 21
house-training, *see* training

Hullock, Mrs N., 21, 22

Immertreu, 21
inertia, 99, 100
Ingram, Mrs and Miss, 29
inoculations, 168

Jacquets Urko, Ch., *134*
Jakeman, Mr G., 21
Jenroy Pop My Cork to Walkon, Ch.,
    28
Jimbren Kennel, 28
Junior Warrant, 141
Juniper of Bramblings, 21

Kennel Club (UK), 44, 67, 148
Kennett, Mrs A., 28
Kinbra Kennels, 28
Kinbra Uncle Sam of Winuwuk, Ch.,
    57
Klansted Kennel, 28
Kluger, Major V., 159
Knowle Crest Kennels, 21
Krey, Mrs M., 156
Kreyons Back in Town (Mack), 24, 156,
    158, *159*, 160, *182*
Kreyons Firebrand, Ch., 156, *161*
Kreyons Kennel, 156

Lacoste von Ellinghaus, *54*
lead training, *see* training
leptospirosis, 168
lice, 171
Liedeberge Kennel, 28
Lounsbury's Flashback Ch., *162*
Lustig von Dom of Tulgey Wood, Ch.,
    20, 21

MacLaren, Mr and Mrs J., 27
Maier's Lord, 16
Malcolm, Mrs J., 24
mange, 171–2
Marbelton Desperate Dan Ch., 26
Marbelton Dressed to Kill, Ch., 26, *62*
Mastiff, 13
mastitis, 97
Mazelaines Texas Ranger, *22*
Mendel, Gregor, 73

Meta v.d. Passage, 14, 17
metritis, 99
Milans Fashion Hint, Int. Ch., *63*, 156
milk failure, 95
Miller, Mr and Mrs W., 28
Ministry of Agriculture, 161
mites, 172
Molossis, 13
Munich Boxer Club, 16, 30

North, Mrs D., 28
Norwatch Brock Buster, Ch., 27, *60*
Norwatch Mustang Wine, 27, *80*
Notelracs Major Beau, Ch., *50*

Panfield Flak, 21
Panfield Kennel, 21, 22, 61
Panfield Serenade, Ch., 21
Panfield Tango, Ch., 21
parasites, 169–72
parvovirus, 168
Perret, Mr P., 28
poisoning, 178
Price, Mrs F., 22
progressive axonopathy (PA), 168
pyometra, 99

Quinto Manalito Von der
    Klappenheide of Marbelton, *55*

Rainey Lane Grand Slam, 24, *79*, 158
Rainey Lane Sirocco, 22
Rayfos Kennel, 28
rescue kennels, 72
retained placenta, 99
Rigo v Angertor, 17
ringworm, 172
road traffic accidents, 173
Rolf von Vogelsberg, Ch., *16*, 18
roundworms, 169, 170

Salgray Kennel, 156
Santanoaks Kennel, 29
sarcoptic mange, 172
Scher Khouns Meshack, Ch., *64*
Scher Khouns Shadrack, Ch., 156, 159
second handling, 133
Seefeld Holbien, CD (Ex), Ch., *10*

Seefeld Kennel, 27, 67
Seefeld Picasso, Ch., 23, *77*
septicaemia, 99
shock, 177
show grooming, 138
show training, *see* training
Sigurd von Dom of Barmere, Int. Ch.,
    18, 20
Skelder Burnt Almond, Ch., 24, *27*
Somerfield, Mrs E., 21, 61
Stainburdorf Kennels, 21
Starmark Sweet Talkin' Guy, Ch., 24,
    61
stewarding, 147
Steynmere Night Rider, Ch., *25*, 26
still birth, 100
stings, bee and wasp, 179
Stockmann, Frau, 18
Summers, Mr M., 22

tapeworms, 169, 170
ticks, 171
Tirkane Kennel, 29
Tonantron Kennels, 28
topping and tailing, *see* handling
Townshend, Mrs J., 29
training, 123–35
    house-training, 123–4
    lead training, 124–6, *135*
    show training, 127–30, *134*
Trywell Kennel, 28
Tyegarth Blue Kiwi, Ch., *48*
Tyegarth Famous Grouse, Ch., 23, *78*
Tyegarth Glenmorangie of Jenroy, Ch.,
    28, *29*

undocked, 104
Utz von Dom of Mazelaine, Int. Ch.,
    19, 20

vaginal discharge, 99
vermifuges, 169
Von Dom Kennel, 18, 21

Wardrobes Clair de Lune, Ch., *25*, 27
Wardrobes Kennel, 22
Wardrobes Miss Mink, Ch., 27
weaning, 105–7

whelping box, 90
white Boxers, *109*, 110, 111
Winkinglight Viking, Ch., 22
Winkinglight Kennels, 21
Winkinglight Justice, Ch., 22
Winuwuk Good Golly, Ch., *24*, 160
Winuwuk Kennel, 67
Winuwuk Milray's Red Baron of
    Valvay, 24, 75, 76, 159, *160, 181*
Witherford Hot Chestnut, Ch., 26, *158*
Witherford Kennel, 26
Withers, Mrs P., 26

worming, 87, 108, 169
Wotan, 17
Wrencliff Flying Scotsman of
    Winuwuk, Ch., *59*
Wrencliff Kennel, 28

Xeno von der Glockenbergen, *51*

Ymar Kennel, 28

Zammit, Mr and Mrs, 29
Zimmerman, Mr P., 22